A Garland Series

The English Stage
Attack and Defense 1577 - 1730

A collection of 90 important works
reprinted in photo-facsimile in 50 volumes

edited by
Arthur Freeman
Boston University

A Defence of the Short View
of the
Profaneness and Immorality
of the English Stage

by

Jeremy Collier

with a preface
for the Garland Edition by

Arthur Freeman

Garland Publishing, Inc., New York & London

1972

Library of Congress Cataloging in Publication Data

Collier, Jeremy, 1650-1726.
    A defence of the Short view of the profaneness and
immorality of the English stage.

    (The English stage: attack and defense, 1577-1730)
    Reprint of the 1699 ed.
    "Wing C5248."
    1. Congreve, William, 1670-1729. Amendments upon
Mr. Collier's false and imperfect citations. 2.
2. Vanbrugh, Sir John, 1664-1726. A short vindication of
The relapse and The provoked wife. 3. Theater--Moral and
religious aspects. 4. Theater--England. I. Title.
II. Series.
PN2047.C62C624 1972   792'.013   72-170444
ISBN 0-8240-0613-5

Printed in the United States of America

Preface

It may be argued that one reason for the persistence and longevity of the controversy over Jeremy Collier's assault on the stage was the eagerness of the initiator to continue and rebut. Following replies by Congreve, Vanbrugh and their "volunteers" Dennis, D'Urfey and Gildon, concurrent with at least three editions of the original Immorality and Profaneness *of 1698, Collier, in the century-old footsteps of Stephen Gosson, offered the earliest of three defenses of his original thesis. First advertised between 8 and 10 November 1698,* A Defence of the Short View *(1699) is addressed principally to Congreve and unfortunately Vanbrugh; a paginary reprint (Lowe 292) was issued in 1705.*

"Since the publishing my late View, &c.," *Collier explains, "I have been plentifully rail'd on in Print." Morality and the good use of rhetoric are again paired, and the attitude of "defence" maintained with Collier's emphatic, colloquial prefatory style: "Some of the* Stage-Advocates

PREFACE

pretend my remarks on their Poetry are forreign to the Business. On the contrary, I conceive it very defensible to disarm an Adversary, if it may be, and disable him from doing mischief . . . the Poets are the Aggressors, let them lay down their Arms first. We have suffer'd under Silence a great while; If we are in any fault, 'tis because we began with them no sooner."

Our reprint is prepared from a copy of the first edition in the possession of the Publishers. It collates $[A]^2 B-I^8 K^6$, $[A]^2$ presumably set with K^6. E3 is mis-signed E5; there are no cancels. Sheets H-K are in type smaller than that of B-G, but there is no clear evidence of shared composition. The errata at the foot of $[A2]^v$ should be noted, especially the first of them.

Wing C 5248; Lowe [1970] 291; Hooker 19. Sister Rose Anthony, pp. 138-147, paraphrases the text.

September, 1971   A. F.

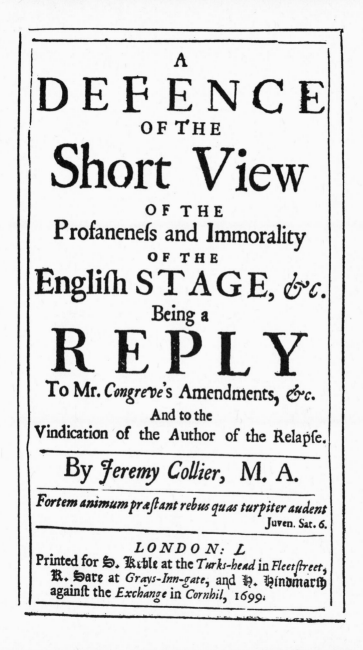

A DEFENCE

OF THE

Short View

OF THE

Profaneness and Immorality

OF THE

English STAGE, &c.

Being a

REPLY

To Mr. *Congreve*'s Amendments, &c.

And to the

Vindication of the Author of the Relapse.

By *Jeremy Collier*, M. A.

Fortem animum præstant rebus quas turpiter audent
Juven. Sat. 6.

LONDON: L
Printed for S. Keble at the *Turks-head* in *Fleetstreet*,
R. Sare at *Grays-Inn-gate*, and H. Hindmarsh
against the *Exchange* in *Cornhil*, 1699.

To the READER.

SInce the publishing my late View, &c. I have been plentifully rail'd on in Print: This gives me some reason to suspect the Answerers and the Cause, are not altogether unlike. Had there been nothing but plain Argument to encounter, I think I might have ventured my Book with them: But being charged with miscitations and unfair Dealing, 'twas requisite to say something: For Honesty is a tender point, and ought not to be neglected.

Mr. Congreve and the Author of the Relapse, being the most eager Complainants, and Principals in the Dispute, I have made it my choice to satisfie them. As for the Volunteers, they will find themselves affected with the Fortune of their Friends; and besides, I may probably have an opportunity of speaking farther with them hereafter.

Notwithstanding the singular Management of the Poets and Play-House, I have had the satisfaction to perceive, the Interest of Virtue is not altogether Sunk, but that Conscience and Modesty have still some Footing among us. This consideration makes me hope a little farther Discovery of the Stage may not be unacceptable. The Reader then may please to take notice, that The Plot and no Plot swears at length, and is scandalously

dalously Smutty and Profane. The Fool in Fashion *for the first four Acts is liable to the same Imputation:* Something in Swearing abated, Cæsar Borgia, *and* Love in a Nunnery, *are no better Complexion'd than the former.* And lastly, Limberham, *and the* Soldier's Fortune, *are meer prodigies of Lewdness and Irreligion. If this general Accusation appears too hard, I am ready to make it good.* 'Twere easy to proceed to many other Plays, *but possibly this Place may not be so proper to enlarge upon the Subject.*

Some of the Stage-Advocates *pretend my Remarks on their Poetry are forreign to the Business. On the contrary, I conceive it very defensible to disarm an Adversary, if it may be, and disable him from doing Mischief.*

To expose that which would expose Religion, *is a warrantable way of Reprizals. Those who* Paint for Debauchery, *should have the Fucus pull'd off, and the Coarseness underneath discover'd. The Poets are the Aggressors, let them lay down their Arms first. We have suffer'd under Silence a great while; If we are in any fault, 'tis because we began with them no sooner*

ERRATA.

PAge 7 l. 15. after represented add, *excepting* Plautus's Amphitryon, *which he calls a Tragecomedy*, p. 19. l. 4. r. summ'd up, p 25. l. 28. r. animos, p. 28. l. 24. after thus dele the comma, p. 31. l. 20. after Indecencies add a Semicolon, l 21. after dealing add a Comma. P 49. l. 21. r. in, p. 59 l 10. r. Mr. Congreve p. 64. l. 29. r. Stile. p. 106. l. 14. for between God and the Devil, r. between his Respects to God and the Devil, p. 114. l. 26. r. say.

AN
ANSWER
TO
Mr. *CONGREVE*s
Amendments, &c.

MR. *Congreve* being a Person of no great Ceremony, I shan't salute him with any Introduction ; but fall to the Business without more Ado. This Gentleman pretends to turn some of my Expressions upon me. *If these Passages*, says he, *produced by* Mr. *Collier* are *obscene* and *profane*, ' why ' are they raked in and disturb'd, unless it ' be to conjure up Vice, and revive Impu-'rities, *&c.* I can't think Mr. *Congreve* so injudicious as to believe this Citation a jot to his purpose. But I plainly perceive he Presumes all along upon the weakness, or partiality of his *Reader :* Which by the way, is no great Compliment.

Amend. p. 5.

B

ment. However, to fay fomething directly. Had *thefe* obnoxious *Paffages* lain hid in a Learned Language, and been lock'd up in Latin, like *Juvenal*, I would no more have let them loofe in a *Tranflation*, than unchain'd the *Tyger* at *Bartholomew Fair* : But fince the Mifchief works in *Englifh*, 'tis time to think of an *Englifh* Remedy. Befides, as to the Smut, I have endeavour'd not to difoblige the *Paper* with any of it. But to fhow the Accufation juft, I made a general Reference to *Play*, and *Character* : And fometimes upon a fpecial Occafion ; have mark'd the *Page*. Indeed to have tranfcrib'd it at length, would not only have been an improper, but a tedious Employment.

I was fenfible the *Poets* would try to make their Advantage, of this Neceffary Referv'dnefs, that They would deny the *Fact*, becaufe the Proof was not particular, and fpoken out. But fince the *Reader* is directed to the Evidence, he may difappoint them in this Evafion, if he pleafes. The profane Part, tho' Bolder, and more Black, will bear the Light better, and therefore when 'twas clear of Obfcenity, I have fet it to the *Bar*. Upon the whole ; I was willing to Guard the Virtue, and awaken the Caution of the *Reader* : And by the fafeft Methods

I

I could think of, to give check to the Complicated Infection.

He affirms I call the *Stage-Poets*, *Buf-* *Amend.* *foons* and *Slaves*; for this he Quotes 81, p. 6. 63, and 175 Pages of the *View*, &c. Let us examine his Proof: The place in the 63 *Page* is a Cenfure of a Profane and Smutty Paffage in the *Old Batchelour*: In which I have faid that *Fondlewife*'s making Sport with Adultery, in the manner defcrib'd, was a Fit of Buffoonry and Profanenefs. Now to fay this of a *Character* in the *Play*, is I fuppofe pretty Different from calling the *Poet* Buffoon. In the 81 *Page*, after I had produced a large Roll of Blafphemy, and *Scripture*-Abufe againft the *Stage*; I thought I had reafon to be fomewhat concern'd; to fee the Chriftian Religion thus horribly outraged, *made the Diverfion* of the *Town*, and the *fcorn* of *Buffoons*: I'm miftaken if this Occafion would not juftify a little feverity of Language: And till Mr. *Congreve* can difprove the Charge, he had much better Repent, than Complain: However there's no neceffity he fhould take that Word to himfelf, unlefs he thinks he deferves it: For it may be applied to the *Actors*, or fome few *Libertines* in the *Audience*, and then his Objection is fpoil'd. His

3*d.* Inftance ftands in *Page* 175*th* of
the *View,* &c. Here upon their unprefi-
dented Familiarity with the *Lords* ; I de-
fired to know whether our *Stage* had *a
particular Privilege ? Was their Charter
enlarg'd*; and were they on the *fame Foot
of Freedom with the Slaves in* the *Saturnalia ?* Here Mr. *Congreve* is pofitive I call
the *Poets Slaves :* 'Tis well when his
Hand was in; He did not charge me
with calling them *Saturnalia :* But which
way do I call them *Slaves?* Why becaufe
I faid, They were very Free. Is Liberty then always faften'd to a Chain ; and
Familiarity a proof of Servitude ? The
Refemblance in the Queftion refpects Behaviour more than Condition, and implies
nothing farther than general Inequality.
Now I hope 'tis no affront to the *Stage,*
to fuppofe them Inferior to the *Houfe of
Lords.* His remaining Inftance from my
Preface, is much like This; and requires
no farther Anfwer.

Thus Mr. *Congreve* may perceive I have
call'd him no *Names* hitherto ; But now
he may be affured I fhould have diftin-
guifh'd his Character a little, and paid
him fome proper Acknowledgments, but
that I have no Inclination for his way of
Difputing : Railing is a mean, and un-
chriftian Talent, and oftentimes a fign of

a

a defperate Caufe, and a defperate Confcience.

As to the bad Imputations thefe *Stage-*
Advocates would throw upon me, I am
not in the leaft difturb'd at Them. I thank
God, they are not only without Truth,
but without Colour. Could They have
made the Slander paffable, we fhould
have heard farther from them. This is
an admirable way of anfwering Books!
All that I fhall fay to't is, that I pity the
Men, and defpife the Malice. To proceed. Mr. *Congreve* is now making *Out-*
works to fortify the Garifon. He lays down
four Rules as the Teft of Criticifm and
Comedy. Thefe He calls *Poftulata*, as if P. 7.
they were Principles of *Science*, and car- P. 12.
ried the Evidence of an *Axiom*. And after he has fpent fome *Pages* in fetting
down thefe Demonftrative Things, he
frankly tells us, they *feem at firft Sight* to
comprehend a *Latitude*. Do they fo? Then Ibid.
they are not Self-evident; They are un-
qualifyed for the Poft he has put them in;
and prove nothing but Sophiftry and Le-
gerdemain. Well! What tho' thefe Rules
are falfe in themfelves, Mr. *Congreve* pro-
mifes to make them True before he has
done with them. For they fhall be fo Ibid.
limited, and *reftrain'd*, and ufed with fuch
Difcretion; that the *Reader* fhall be per-

fectly indemnifyed. However, I can't help suspecting these fair Words: For if He intends to deal clearly, why does he make the Touchstone faulty, and the Standard uncertain? For these reasons, I must examine for my Self; And since he owns his *Propositions* not evidently true, I'll try if I can't prove the greatest part of them evidently false.

To begin with him. His Latitude of *Comedy* upon *Aristotle*'s Definition; as he Explains it, wont pass without Limitation. For

P. 7.

1*st*. His Construction of Μίμησις Φαυλοτέςων is very questionable. These Words may as properly be Translated the *Common*, as *the worst Sort of People*. And thus *Hesychius* interprets Φϋλ☺ by ἰυτελής.

2*ly*. *Comedy* is distinguish'd from *Tragedy* by the Quality of the Persons, as well as by other Circumstances. *Aristotle* informs us that the Appearance, Characters, or Persons are greater in *Tragedy*, than in *Comedy*. Τὰ σχήματα μείζω καὶ ἰντιμότερα. And to this Sense *Petitus* interprets the Words Βελτίοραη ἤ χείςοναι, affirming they ought to relate to Quality, as well as Manners.

Lib. de Poet. cap. 4.

In not. ad Lib. Arist. de Poet. cap. 2.

Now as the Business of *Tragedy* is to represent Princes and Persons of Quality; so by the Laws of Distinction, *Comedy* ought

ought to be confin'd to the ordinary
Rank of Mankind. And that *Aristotle* Scalig.
ought to be thus interpreted appears from Lib. 1. c.6.
the Form of *New Comedy*, set up in the
Time of this Philosopher. And tho' we
have none of these *Comedies* extant, 'tis
agreed by the Criticks that they did not
meddle with Government and Great People; The *Old Comedy* being put down upon this Score. And tho' *Menander* and
the rest of that Set are lost, we may guess
at their Conduct from the Plays of *Plautus* and *Terence*, in all which there is not
so much as one Person of Quality represented.

Farther, Mr. *Congreve*'s Reason why
Aristotle should be interpreted by *Manners*, and not *Quality* is inconclusive. His
remark on κατὰ πᾶσαν κακίαν will serve as
well the other way. Lets try it a little :
Aristotle shall say then that *Comedy* is an
imitation of the ordinary, and middle sort
of People, but not κατὰ πᾶσαν κακίαν, *in every branch and aggravation of Vice*; for as Amend.
Mr. *Congreve* observes, *there are Crimes too* p. 8.
daring and too horrid for Comedy. Now I
desire to know, if this Sense is not clear
and unembarrass'd, if it does not distinguish *Comedy* from *Tragedy* , and bring
down the Definition to Matter of Fact?

But

But granting Mr. *Congreve* his Definition ; all Blemishes and Instances of Scandal are not fit to make sport with. Co-
vetousness, and Profusion ; Cowardize,
Spleen, and Singularity, well managed,
might possibly do. But some Vices Mr.
Congreve confesses *are too daring for Comedy.* Yes and for *Tragedy* too. And among
these I'll venture to say Profaneness is one.
This Liberty even *Aristotle* durst not allow : He knew the Government of *A-
thens* would not endure it. And that

Vit.Eurip. some of the *Poets* had been call'd to ac-
Ed. Cant. count upon this Score.

2*ly*. Immodesty and lewd Talking, is
another part of Vice which ought not to
appear in *Comedy*. *Aristotle* blames the
Old Comedians for this sort of Mismanage-
ment; and adds,that intemperate Rallying

See ought to lie under publick Restraint. And
View, &c. therefore Mr. *Congreve* is mistaken in his
p. 159. Consequence if he makes it general. For
160. *the looser sort of Livers* , as to the Foul-

Amend. ness of Conversation , are no proper *Sub-*
p. 8. *ject of Comedy.*

But supposing *Aristotle* more liberal to
Mr. *Congreve*, what service would it do
him ? Does not Christianity refine the
Pleasures , and abridge the Liberties of

Ephes. 5. *Heathenism?* St. *Paul* bids us *put away all*
3, 4. *filthyness and foolish talking,* and that such
things

things *ought not so much as to be named* Colof. 3. 8. *amongst Christians.* And when *Revelation* says one thing, and *Paganism* another, how are we to determine? Is not an *Apostle's* Testimony more cogent than that of a Philosopher, and the *New Testament* above all the Rules of *Aristotle* and *Horace*?

Thus we see his first *Postulatum* is far from being true in the Generality stated by him.

Before I part with him on this Head, I can't but take notice of his saying, that P. 8. *the Business of Comedy is to delight, as well as instruct*: If he means as much, by *as well,* he is mistaken. For Delight is but View, &c. the secondary End of *Comedy,* as I have cap. 4. prov'd at large. And to satisfy him farther, I'll give him one Testimony more of Mr. *Dryden's.* 'Tis in his *Preface* to *Fresnoy's Art of Painting.* Here he informs P. xx. us that as to Delight *the parallel of the* (two) *Arts holds true; with this difference; That the principal End of Painting is to please, and the chief design of Poetry is to instruct.*

Thus Mr. *Congreve's* first Rule signifies little ; And therefore his *Second* being, but a consequence of it, must fall of Course. *Pleasure,* especially the Pleasure of *Libertines,* is not the Supreme *Law* of *Comedy.*

Vice

Vice muſt be under Diſcipline and Diſcountenance, and Folly ſhown with great
Caution and Reſerve. Luſſious Deſcrip-
tions, and Common Places of Lewdneſs
are unpardonable. They affront the virtuous, and debauch the unwary, and are
a ſcandal to the Country where they are
ſuffer'd. The pretence of *Nature*, and
Imitation, is a lamentable Plea. Without doubt there's a great deal of *Nature*
in the moſt brutal Practices. The infamous *Stews* 'tis likely talk in their own
way, and keep up to their Character. But
what Perſon of probity would viſit them
for their Propriety, or take Poyſon becauſe 'tis true in its kind? All Characters
of Immodeſty (if there muſt be any ſuch)
ſhould only be hinted in remote Language, and thrown off in Generals.

If there muſt be Strumpets, let *Bridewell*
be the *Scene*. Let them come not to Prate,
but to be Puniſh'd. To give Succeſs, and
Reputation to a *Stage Libertine*, is a ſign
either of Ignorance, of Lewdneſs, or A-
theiſm, or altogether. Even thoſe Inſtances which will bear the relating ought to
be puniſh'd. But as for Smut and Profaneneſs, 'tis every way Criminal and Infectious, and no Diſcipline can atone for
the Repreſentation: When a *Poet* will
venture on theſe Liberties, his *Perſwaſion*
must

Amend.
p. 11.

muſt ſuffer, and his *private Sentiments* fall under Cenſure. For as Mr. *Dryden* rightly obſerves, *vita proba eſt*, is no excuſe: For *'twill ſcarcely be admitted that either a Poet or a Painter can be chaſt, who give us the contrary Examples in their Writings, and their Pictures.* I agree with Mr. *Congreve it would be very hard a Painter ſhould be believ'd to reſemble all the ugly Faces he draws.* But if he ſuffers his Pencil to grow Licentious, if he gives us Obſcenities, the Merits of *Raphael* won't excuſe him: No, To do an ill Thing well, doubles the Fault. The Miſchief riſes with the Art, and the Man ought to ſmart in proportion to his Excellency : 'Tis one of the Rules in Painting according to Mr. *Dryden* and *Freſnoy*; To *avoid every Thing that's immoral and filthy, unſeemly, impudent, and obſcene.* And Mr. *Dryden* continues, that a Poet is bound up to the ſame Reſtraint, and ought neither to *Deſign,* or *Colour* an offenſive Piece.

Pref. to *Freſnoy.* p. XXI.

Pref. p. XX. Book. p. 56.

Ibid. p. XXI.

Mr. *Congreve*'s 4*th* Propoſition relates to the *Holy Scriptures* ; And here he endeavours to Fence againſt the Cenſure of Profaneneſs. He deſires the following Diſtinction *may be admitted,* viz. *when Words are applied to ſacred Things, they ought to be underſtood accordingly: But when they are otherwiſe applied, the Diverſity of the Sub-*

Amend. p. 11.

ject

ject gives a Diverfity of Signification : **By**
his favour this Diſtinction is loofe, and
nothing to the Purpofe. The inſpired
Text is appropriated to *Sacred Things*,
and never to be ufed but upon ferious Occafions. The Weight of the Matter, and
the Dignity of the Author, challenge our
utmoſt regard. 'Tis only for the Service
of the *Sanctuary*, and Privileged from common Ufe. But Mr. *Congreve* fays *when
they* (the Words of Scripture) *are other-
wife applied, the Diverfity of the Subject
gives a Diverfity of Signification*. This is
ſtrange Stuff! Has Application fo tranf-
forming a Quality, and does bare ufe enter fo far into the Nature of Things? If
a Man applies his Money to an ill Purpofe,
does this tranfmute the Metal, and make
it none of the Kings Coin ? To wreſt an
Author, and turn his Words into Jeſt,
is it feems to have nothing to do with
him. The meer Ridicule deſtroys the
Quotation ; and makes it belong to another Perfon. Thus 'tis impoſſible to Tra-
verſtie a Book, and *Virgil* was never burlefqu'd by *Aufonius* or Mr. *Cotton* ! Not
at all ! They only made ufe of the 24
Letters, and happen'd to chop exactly upon *Virgil*'s Subject, his Words and Ver-
ſification. But 'tis plain they never intended to quote him : For *Virgil* is always

ways grave, and serious, but these Gentle-
men apply, or translate the Words in the
most different manner imaginable : And
run always upon Buffoonry and Drolling.
This is Mr. *Congreve*'s Logick, and to abuse
an Author is to have nothing to do with
him. The Injury it seems destroys the
Relation, and makes the Action perfectly foreign. And by this Reasoning one
would think my Book had never been
cited by Mr. *Congreve*.

To illustrate the Matter a little farther. Suppose the most solemn Acts
of Government play'd the Fool with at
Bartholomew Fair; The Judges *Charge*
made up into a *Farce*, and the *Poppets* re-
peating an *Act of Parliament* : Would it
be a good excuse to alledge they meant
nothing but a little Laughing. That the
Bench and the *Bear-Garden*, *Punchinello*
and the 2 *Houses*, had the *same Alphabet
in Common*? That they ought to have
the Privilege of Speech, and put their
Words together as they had a mind to :
Would not the Reason, and the Hardi-
ness of such a Plea, be very extraordinary? The Case before us is much the
same, only a great deal worse. For what
can be more outrageously Wicked, than
to expose Religion to the Scorn of A-
theism, to give up the Bible to *Rakes* and
Strumpets,

Old Batch.
p. 39. 49.

Love for
Love. p. 59.
61.
Double
Dealer. p.
18, &c.
Strumpets, and to make Impudence and Inspiration speak the same Language? Thus the Wisdom of God is burlesqu'd, his Omnipotence play'd with, and Heaven's the Diversion of Hell. To reply, that tho' the *Words are Scripture, the Subject and Application are different,* is to confess the Indictment, and give up the Cause. For pray what is it to burlesque a grave Author? Is it not to wrest his Meaning, and alter his Matter; to turn him into Jest and Levity, and put him under Circumstances of Contempt?

Thus we see his *4th* Proposition is all Sophistry, and false Reasoning:

I shall now go back to his *3d*, which I think would have stood as well in the last place. He *desires the impartial Reader, not to consider any Expression or Passage, cited from any Play, as it appears in* P. 9, 10. my Book; *nor to pass any Sentence upon it out of its proper Scene,* &c. For it must not be medled with *when 'tis alienated from its Character.* Well! Let the *Reader* compare his *Plays* with the *View,* &c. as much as he pleases. However, there's no necessity of passing through all his Forms, and Methods of prescribing. For if the Passage be truly cited, if the Sentence be full, and determin'd, why mayn't we understand it where'ere 'tis met with? Why

Why muſt we read a Page for a Period?
Can't a Plant be known without the
Hiſtory of the Garden? Beſides, He may
remember I have frequently hinted his
Characters, touched upon their Quality
and Fortune, and made them an Aggravation of his Fault.

But to ſilence this Plea, I had told
him before that no pretence of Character,
or Puniſhment, could juſtify Profaneneſs
on the *Stage*. I gave him my Reaſons View.
for't too, which he is not pleas'd to take p. 96.
notice of. To enlarge on them a little:

And here I deſire to know what Service does Blaſphemy, and Profaneneſs upon the *Stage*? Is it to pleaſe, or to improve the Audience? Surely not the firſt:
For what Pleaſure can it be to ſee the
greateſt Being contemn'd, the beſt Friend
ill treated, and the ſtrongeſt Enemy provok'd? The *Jews* uſed to rend their
Cloaths at the hearing of Blaſphemy, and
is it now become the Entertainment of
Chriſtians? To ſee Men defy the Almighty, and play with Thunder, one
would think ſhould be far from Diverſion. Are the Charms of Profaneneſs ſo
ſtrangely inviting, is there ſuch Muſick
in an Oath, and are the Damn'd to be
courted for their Company? The *Stage*
is oftentimes a lively Emblem of Hell;
There's

There's the Language, and the **Lewd-**
ness; There are the Devils too, and almost every thing but the Darkness and
Despair. These hideous Characters are
generally Persons of Figure, often re-
warded, seldom punish'd, and when they
are, the Correction is strangely gentle and
disproportion'd. 'Tis just as if a Man
should be set in the *Stocks* for Murther,
and shamed a little for firing a Town.

To say a Man has been Profane in general, and then to punish him is somewhat Intelligible; To make him an Example without Instance, and Particulari-
ty, is a safe way of Dramatick Justice:
But when he is suffer'd to Act his Distraction, and practise before the Company,
the Punishment comes too late. Such
Malefactors are infectious, and kill at
their very Execution. 'Tis much safer
not to hear them talk, than to see them
suffer. A bad Age is too apt to learn;
and the Punishment in jest, brings on
the Crime in earnest. Some Vices won't
bear the naming: They are acted in some
measure when they are spoken, and ap-
prov'd when they are hearkn'd to. Thus
the *Play-House* often spreads those Vices
it represents, and the Humour of the
Town is learn'd by shewing it. So that if
Instruction is intended, nothing can be
more

more Ignorant, if Diversion nothing more
Wicked. To proceed. Profaneness by being often heard, is less abhorr'd. The
aversion cools upon Custom, and the
frightfulness of the Idea is abated. Familiarity reconciles us to ill Sights, and
wears off the Deformity of a Monster.
Thus by Cursing and Swearing, the Abuse
of *Scripture* and Profane Jests, which are
so frequent on the *Stage*, the Boldness of
the Crime grows less remarkable, and
the Terrors of Conscience are laid asleep:
And if there happens to be Wit in the
Case, 'tis a Vehicle to the Poyson, and
makes it go down with Pleasure. Thus
young People are furnished with Profane
Jests, and Atheism is kept in Countenance:
The Majesty of Religion is weaken'd, and
the Passions of Humane Nature misplaced:
People laugh when they should tremble,
and despise what they ought to adore.
Had we a due regard for the Honour of
God, and were Death and Judgment laid
before us, that is, were we Christians in
good earnest; these wretched Liberties
would be all Pain, and Pennance to us:
They'd wound the Sense, and chill the
Blood, and make us sweat with Antipathy
and Disgust: We should be seiz'd with
a fit of Horror, and almost frighten'd into Agony and Convulsion.

C   From

From what I have said 'twill follow, that provided Mr. *Congreve* is fairly cited for Smut, or Profaneneſs, *Sentence may be paſſed* without having recourſe to *Scene*, or *Character*. I ſay it may be paſſed ſo far as to condemn him of a Fault; Tho' I confeſs the degrees, and aggravation of it, will in ſome meaſure depend on the *Characters*, and the Fortune of them.

I have done with Mr. *Congreve*'s Pre-liminaries, and ſhown the unreaſonable-neſs of them. If he demands them as a Right, his Title is defeated, if he begs them as a Favour, he ſhould have peti-tion'd in another Form. He ſhould not have been ſo ſhort with the *Reader* as to *deſire him to proceed no farther, but return to my View*, &c. *if he thought in his Con-ſcience his few things too much to be granted.* But why ſhould this Gentleman put this hardſhip upon People, which he does not allow of himſelf? I ſuppoſe Mr. *Congreve*'s Conſcience may be large enough for any *Reader*, why then does he require any more? The Author thinks his *few things, too much* to be granted, and yet the *Cour-teous Reader* muſt think otherwiſe! I ſay Mr. *Congreve* thinks them *too much*, why elſe does he engage to uſe them with ſuch Caution, to muzzle, and bind them up to their good Behaviour?

Mr.

Amend.
P. 7.

P. 12.

Mr. *Congreve* proceeds to acquaint us how careful the *Stage* is for the *Inſtruction* of the *Audience.* That *the Moral of the* P. 12, 13. *whole is generally ſumm'd in the concluding Lines of the Poem, and put into Rhyme that it may be eaſy and engaging to the Memory.* To this I anſwer,

1*ſt.* That this *Expedient* is not always made uſe of. And not to trouble the *Reader* with *many* Inſtances, we have nothing of it in *Love in a Nunnery,* and the *Relapſe,* both which *Plays* are in my Opinion not a little dangerous.

2*ly.* Sometimes theſe Comprehenſive Lines do more harm than good : They do ſo in *the Souldiers Fortune :* They do ſo likewiſe in the *Old Batchelour ;* which inſtructs us to admirable purpoſe in theſe Words;

But oh ------

What rugged ways attend the Noon of Life ?
(Our ſun declines) and with what anxious ſtrife,
What pain we tug that galling Load a Wife ?

This Moral is uncourtly, and vitious, it encourages Lewdneſs, and agrees extreamly well with the *Fable. Love for Love* may have ſomewhat a better Farewel, but would do a Man little Service
ſhould

should he remember it to his dying Day. Here *Angelica* after a fit of Profane Vanity in *Prose*, takes her Leave as follows;

> *The Miracle to Day is that we find*
> *A Lover true : Not that a Woman's kind.*

This last Word is somewhat ambiguous, and with a little help may strike off into a light Sense. But take it at the best, 'tis not overloaden with Weight and Apothegme. A *Ballad* is every jot as sententious.

3*dly*. Supposing the Moral grave, and unexceptionable, it amounts to little in the present Case. Alas! The Doctor comes too late for the Disease, and the Antidote is much too weak for the Poyson. When a *Poet* has flourished on an ill Subject for some Hours : When he has Larded his *Scenes* with Smut, and play'd his Jests on Religion ; and exhausted himself upon Vice ; what can a dry Line or two of good Counsel signify ? The Tincture is taken, the Fancy is preingaged, and the Man is gone off into another Interest. Profane Wit, Luscious Expressions, and the handsome Appearance of a *Libertine*, solicit strongly for Debauchery. These Things are mighty Recruits to Folly, and make the Will too hard for the Understanding.

ftanding. A tafte of Philofophy has a very flat relifh, after fo full an Entertainment. An agreeable Impreffion is not
eafily defaced by a fingle Stroak, efpecially when 'tis worn deep by Force, and
Repetition. And as the *Audience* are not
fecur'd, fo neither are the Poets this way.
A Moral Sentence at the Clofe of a Lewd
Play, is much like a pious Expreffion in
the Mouth of a dying Man, who has
been Wicked all his Life time. This fome
ignorant People call making a good End,
as if one wife Word would attone for an
Age of Folly. To return to the *Stage*.
I fuppofe other parts of a Difcourfe befides the Conclufion, ought to be free
from Infection. If a Man was Sound only at his Fingers Ends, he would have
little comfort in his Conftitution. *Bonum
fit ex integra caufa*; A good Action muft
have nothing bad. The Quality muft be
uniform, and reach to every Circumftance.
In fhort. This Expedient of Mr. *Congreve's* as 'tis infignificant to the purpofe
'tis brought, fo it looks very like a piece
of formal Hypocricy: And feems to be
made ufe of to conceal the Immorality of
the *Play*, and cover the *Poet* from Cenfure.

Mr. *Congreve* in the *Double Dealer* makes
three of his Ladies Strumpets; This, I
thought

thought an odd Compliment to *Quality*.
But my Reflection it feems is over fevere.
However, by his favour, the Characters
in a *Play* ought to be drawn by Nature:
To write otherwife is to make a Farce.
The *Stage* therefore muft be fuppos'd an
Image of the World, and Quality in Fiction refemble Quality in Life. This
Refemblance fhould likewife hold in
Number, as well as in other Refpects,
tho' not to a Mathematical Strictnefs.
Thus in *Plautus* and *Terence*, the *Slaves*
are generally reprefented falfe, and the
Old Men eafy and over credulous. Now
if the Majority in thefe Divifions fhould
not anfwer to the *World* ; If the *Drama*
fhould crofs upon *Converfation*, the *Poets*
would be to blame, as I believe they are
in the later Inftance. Thus when the
greateft part of *Quality* are debauched on
the *Stage*, 'tis a broad *Innuendo* they are
no better in the *Boxes*.

This Argument he pretends proves too
much, and would make us believe that
by this way of reafoning, *if four Women
were fhewn upon the Stage, and three of them
were Vitious, it is as much as to fay that three
parts in four of the whole Sex are ftark naught.*
P. 16.   I anfwer, the Cafe is not parallel. The
Reprefentation in his *Play* turns more upon Condition than Sex. 'Tis the *Quali-*
ty

ty which makes the Appearance, marks the *Character*, and points out to the Comparison Abroad.

His Precedents from *Virgil* are unserviceable upon two Accounts.

1*st.* The Fact is misreported. The Catalogue of ill Women in that *Poem*, is not so numerous as is pretended. Mr. *Congreve* exempts four of them from this Charge, and I'll help him to four more. For *Creusa* and *Lavinia* are perfectly passive; and over-ruled. Then as for *Camilla*, why is she Thrown into the black List, and ranged with *Alecto* and the *Harpyes*? What *Decrees of the Gods does she despise*? She stood by *Latinus* 'tis true, neither does the *Poet* oblige her to quit his Interest. So that for any thing that appears, the Lady was a good Woman in her way. To these if we add *Anna*, *Dido's* Sister, a very innocent Princess, I beleive we may venture to Poll with *Juno*, and all her Party.

2*ly.* His Matter of Fact as stated by himself, makes against him. For if *Virgil* did well in making most of his Female Characters faulty and exceptionable, be- *Congr.* cause as *Aristotle has ventur'd to affirm,* P. 17 *there are more bad than good Women in the World*, then there ought to be a proportion between Life and poetick Imitation ;

C 4   A

A Proportion even to Computation, tho'
not juſt to equality and telling of Noſes.
And thus his Illuſtration deſtroys his Argument, even by the Authority of *Ariſtotle* and *Boſſu*; and which is worſt of all,
by his own, who cites them with Approbation.

There's one unlucky thing behind: And
that is his concurring with *Ariſtotle* in a
very unceremonious Paradox. This Philoſopher *has ventur'd to affirm that there
are more bad, than good Women in the World.*
Very likely? If he had ſaid there are more
bad Men than good ones, the Diſcovery
might have been altogether as conſiderable. But we are not yet at the end of the
Indictment. For as he goes on, *The Women* (take them altogether) *do more harm
than good.* Well. *Ariſtotle* was a bold Man:
However, this is to be ſaid for him; he
was no *Stage Poet*. Had his concerns been
with the *Pit* or *Boxes*, 'tis likely you had
ſeen him better poliſh'd. But that Mr.
Congreve ſhould Countenance an Author
in his Misbehaviour, and make his Court,
thus awkardly to the Ladies, is ſomewhat
ſurprizing. Is this the way to oblige the
Women, to tell them *they do more harm
than good in the World*; that their Sex is a
Publick Nuſance, and an Errour in Creation?

Ibid.

Ibid.

I had charg'd our Modern Dramatists, and particularly Mr. *Congreve* with being too free in expoſing the Nobility under Characters of Lewdneſs and Contempt. This I obſerv'd was no Cuſtom of the *Roman Stage*; And that *Plautus* and *Terence*, were much more courtly and reſerv'd. This Remark he endeavours to diſprove from *Perſius* and *Juvenal*. As how? Did theſe Authors write either *Comedy* or *Tragedy*, or have their Citations any Reference to the *Drama*? Not at all: Why then are they alledg'd? To what End is a foreign Character and Buſineſs haled in to determine upon the *Stage*? Well. But theſe *Poets* were Satyriſts, and play'd their Invectives upon *Quality*, and is not this ſomewhat to the purpoſe? But very little. For,

View. p. 12, 175
Amend. p. 19.

1*ſt*. The Satyr of a *Comedian* and another *Poet*, have a different Effect upon Reputation. A Character of Diſadvantage upon the *Stage*, makes a ſtronger Impreſſion than elſewhere. Reading is but Hearing at the ſecond Hand: Now Hearing at the beſt, is a more languid Conveyance than Sight. For as *Horace* obſerves,

Segnius irritant animios demiſſa per aurem,
Quam quæ ſunt oculis ſubjecta fidelibus. —

De. Art: Poet.

The

The Eye is much more affecting, and strikes deeper into the Memory than the Ear. Besides, Upon the *Stage* both the Senses are in Conjunction. The Life of the Action fortifies the Object, and awakens the Mind to take hold of it. Thus a dramatick Abuse is rivetted in the *Audience*, a Jest is improv'd into an Argument, and rallying grows up into Reason: Thus a Character of Scandal becomes almost indelible, a Man goes for a Blockhead upon *Content*; and he that's made a Fool in a *Play*, is often made one for his Lifetime. 'Tis true he passes for such only amongst the prejudiced and unthinking; but these are no inconsiderable Division of Mankind. For these Reasons, I humbly conceive the *Stage* stands in need of a great deal of Discipline and Restraint: To give them an unlimited Range, is in effect to make them Masters of all Moral Distinctions, and to lay Honour and Religion at their Mercy. To shew Greatness ridiculous, is the way to lose the use, and abate the value of the Quality. Things made little in jest, will soon be so in earnest: For Laughing and Esteem, are seldom bestow'd on the same Object.

2*ly.* The Censures of *Juvenal* and *Persius*, are very moderate, and remote in Mr. *Congreve*'s Citations. *Juvenal* comes some-

somewhat the clofeſt. He Rallies the Flattery and Partiality of the Times; and tells us that Gaming & Debauchery were Scandalous to little People; But when theſe Vices dwelt in great Houſes, they chang'd Complexion, and grew *Modiſh* and *Gentile.* Thus we ſee the *Poet* keeps within the Terms of Reſpect, ſlides over the *Quality*, and points rather upon the *Fortune* of the Libertine. Now had *Juvenal* written a *Comedy*, laid the Scene in his own Country, Created a Lord a *Coxcomb*, and ſhewn him ſuch for three hours together, his caſe had been ſomewhat hard. But this branch of *Satyr* was left for Mr. *Congreve*'s refining; who to do him right, has treated the Character with *much Delicacy of fine Raillery, and Excellency of Good Manners*, as he Phraſes it.

Double Dealer.

Amend. P. 27.

His Teſtimony from *Rapin* does not come up to his Point. For as I obſerv'd, *Moliere* Ridicules no Quality higher than a *Marquis* : Now, notwithſtanding Mr. *Dennis*'s Exclamation, a *Marquis* in *France* is much leſs than a *Marquis* in *England*, or a *Baron* either. This I take it is pretty plain from *Moliere* himſelf, for in his Play called, *L' Impromtu de Verſailles, Brecourt* one of the Minor Nobleſs, treats a *Marquis* with great Familiarity. He calls him *Mon puavre Marquis*, and *Je te promet*

View, &c. p. 175.

P. 22. 29.

Mar-

Marquis ; now this way of speaking is not Manners, unless to Equals, or Inferiors.

And in another Play, the *Chevalier Dorante* Converses with a *Marquis* upon Terms of Equality, and *Climene* a Lady, salutes him only by the Title of *Monsieur*, whereas *Monseigneur* belongs to the Quality of an *English* Lord. The *Orders* of the Bishop of *Arras* run in this Stile; And so likewise does the Address of two *French* Letters to the present Ld. Bishop of *London*, printed at the end of a Book called the *Unreasonableness of Separation*. Farther, *Rapin* seems to Cite *L' Impromptu* above-mentioned. Here *Meliere* informs us, that whereas Comedy formerly plaid the Fool with none but Slaves and Serving-men, now the Case was alter'd, and there was no sport without a ridiculous *Marquis*. But as for making bold *with People of Quality and the Court*, this is all added by *Rapin*. However, granting this, the meaning and practice of *Moliere*, 'tis easily reconciled with the Sense I am contending for. For a Person of Quality does not sound so high in *French* as in *English*; the lower Nobless being often comprehended in this Distinction. Thus *Moliere*'s *Brecourt* is called a Man of Quality in the List of the *Characters*,

but

Critique de Escole des Femmes. p. 286, 287.

View, &c. P. 245.

L' Impromptu. &c.

but in the *Play* he is only *Chevalier*, or a Knight, at the beſt.   And in his Play, called, *L' Bourgeois Gentil-Homme*, a Perſon of Quality often means no more than a Gentleman.   And to proceed, thus we may fairly underſtand the remainder of *Rapin* in Mr. *Congreve's* Citation.   He tells us the other *Poets Play'd only upon Common and Country Converſation, in their Comedies, Et* Moliere *a joue tout* Paris *et la Cour. La Cour*, yes; but not *toute la Cour*. Here *Rapin* oppoſes, *La vie Bourgeoiſe,* Country Converſation, to the *Court.*   Now *un* Bourgeoiſe ſignifies a Perſon of the *Third Eſtate*, as diſtinguiſhed from the *Nobleſs,* or *Gentry.*   So that the meaning of the Paſſage ſeems to be no more, than that *Moliere* took ſome of his *Fools* from the *Gentry,* which was more than the *Stage* had done before.   But after all, if *Rapin* has mis-reported *Moliere,* and given him more Liberty than he took, it makes no-thing to Mr. *Congreve's* purpoſe; for the force of the Teſtimony does not lye in what *Rapin* has ſaid, but in what *Moliere* has written.

Mr. *Congreve* is ſo hardy as to affirm that *I am in plain terms for having Com-plements paſs'd on Perſons of Quality, and nei-ther will allow their Follies, nor their Vi-ces to be expoſed.*   This I confeſs is to be

over-

P. 15. 31.
& alib.

Furetiere.

over - Ceremonious. But the best on't is, there's nothing like it in the whole Book. The very place quoted by Mr. *Congrieve* is a proof of the Calumny: The Passage stands in the Form of a question thus. *And can't they lash the Vice, without pointing upon the Quality?* Which way of speaking, supposes it a very practicable business; unless this Gentleman will affirm that *Folly*, and *Peerage*, are Inseparable. I would gladly know what over-straining of Ceremony, What Flatery is there in all this? I confess, I am of Opinion that all *Satyr* ought to have regard to Quality and Condition, and that Decency and Reproof should go together. I can't think it any *Excellence of good Manners*, to expose the *Nobility* in their *Robes*, to put Contempt among their Titles, and to represent them in such a Manner, as if the Lord and the Fool, like Horse and Man, in a *Centaur*, grew naturally together.

Mr. *Congreve* proceeds in his Defence, and endeavors to wipe off the Imputation of *Smut* and *Pedantry* from Ld. *Touchwood*; But here he Cites more than is necessary: I had nothing to do with his *Verses*, as the Reader may easily Imagine. 'Twas the *Prose part* of Ld. *Touchwood* to which I Objected. And that I say still is foul

(marginal notes:)
View, &c.
p. 175.

Double Dealer
p. 79.
Amend.
p. 22.

foul in the Image, Embarrass'd with trifling Epithites, and ill suited to the Character. But thus by producing the Innocent with the Guilty, he hoped to make
the Charge appear unreasonable.

We are now come to the *Mourning-
Bride*, and Mr. *Congreve* seems so well as-
sur'd of the Decency of this *Play*, that he
casts the whole Cause upon it. *If there be
Immodesty in this Tragedy* (says he) *I must
confess my self incapable of ever writing any
thing with Modesty*. It may be so: An ill
Custom is very hard to Conquer, with
some People. But setting this matter
aside; I still charge Mr. *Congreve* with
Immodesty; 'tis in *Osmin's* last Speech in
the *Page* above-mentioned. Indeed I did
not Cite the words because I am not willing to furnish the Reader with a Collection of Indecencies, to shew I design
nothing but fair dealing: I always refer
to the *Play*, and generally to the Character, and *Page*, where such Entertainment is to be met with. This is pressing
the Charge as far as the Case will bear;
But because the Passages are unfit to be
shown, Mr. *Congreve* and his Brethren
deny the Fact: A great Instance of their
Modesty in another Sense. Is it Innocence then to be guilty of things too bad
to be nam'd? What sort of Faults must
those

Amend. p. 23.

M. Bride, p. 36.

those be, which won't endure the Light,
tho only to punish them.

This Gentleman quarrels with me because I would have had *Almeria* and *Of-*
min parted *Civilly*; as if it was not proper for Lovers to do so: But *Civility*, and
Incivility have nothing to do with Paſſion.
I deny that, *Incivility* and *Paſſion*, are
often concern'd together; And I ſuppoſe
his *Amendments* may make an Inſtance.

By *Civilly*, I meant only decently, as
any one might eaſily imagine. And as
for *Tenderneſs*, when it grows Rank, and
Nauſeous, 'tis Rudeneſs, I take it.

Mr. *Congreve* would excuſe *Oſmin*'s
Rant, by ſaying, *That moſt of the Inci-*
dents of the Poem of this Scene and the for-
mer, were laid to prepare for the Violence
of theſe Expreſſions. If it be ſo, I think
the Play was not worth the Candle. 'Tis
much as Wiſe as it would be for a Man
to make a long Preparation to get out of
his Wits, and qualifie himſelf for *Bedlam.*
For nothing can be more diſtracted than
Oſmin. He is for *riving his clotted Hair,*
Smearing the Walls with his Blood, and daſh-
ing his disfigured Face againſt ſomething.
And a great deal more ſuch ſtuff, as a
Man may go to all the Mad-Houſes in
Town, and ſcarcely hear of. Was it
worth *Oſmin*'s while to be thus Crazy,
and

Amend. p.
24.

Ibid.

M. Bride
P. 36.

and are all Lovers to take a Pattern from this *Hero*? I am sorry Mr. *Congreve* was at all this trouble for a Prophane Allusion; but he is positive there's nothing *either of Prophaneness or Immodesty in the Expression.* Amend. With *Immodesty* I did not Charge it: But P. 25. is there nothing of *Profaneness* in bringing the most solemn Things in Religion upon the *Stage*; In making a Mad-man Rave about *Heaven*, and in comparing the disappointments of Love, with *Damnation*? The Lines shall appear once again.

> *O my* Almeria;
> *What do the Damn'd endure but to despair;*
> *But knowing Heaven to know it lost for ever!*

Mr. *Congreve* does not know how *these* P. 26. *Verses are a Similitude drawn from the Creed:* I can't help it. I thought the Eternal Punishment of the Damned had been part Athanas. of of the *Creed*. I shan't untie such knots Creed. as these are for the future. He tells me *I had but an ill hold of Profaneness in his Play, and was reduced to catch at the Poetry*; And then makes a miserable jest about *Corruption* Ibid. and *Generation. I had but ill hold of Profaneness!* As ill as 'twas, he has not yet wrested it from me. 'Twas in my Power besides to have taken better, and since he complains of gentle usage, I shall do it. D In

M. *Bride*
P. 8, 9, 29,
41, 48.

In the firſt place, here's frequent Swearing *by Heaven*; I ſuppoſe the *Poets* think
this nothing, their *Plays* are ſo much larded with it. But our *Saviour* has given
us an other Notion of this Liberty; He
charges us *not to Swear at all*. And tells

Sc. Mat. 5.
34. xxiii.
22.

us expreſsly, that *He that ſwears by Hea-*
ven, ſwears by the Throne of God, and by
him that ſits thereon.

To go on to another Branch of his
Irreligion. The Scene of this *Play* lies in
Chriſtendom, as is evident from the Hi-

P. 36.

ſtory, or Fable; and to mention nothing
more from *Oſmin*'s Rant: Let us ſee then
how *Oſmin* accoſts *Almeria*, when he found
her ſafe on Shore: Truly I think their
Meeting is as extravagant, as their *Part-*

Amend.
P. 24.

ing, tho Mr. *Congreve* won't allow it
ſhould be ſo. The Ceremony runs thus.

Mourn. B.
P. 19.

Thou Excellence, thou Joy, thou Heaven of
Love.

Thus the little ſucceſſes of a pair of Lovers, are equall'd with the Glories of
Heaven; And a Paultry Paſſion ſtrain'd
up to the Beatifick Viſion. I ſay Pal-
try, for ſo 'tis upon the Compariſon.
To go on. *Almeria* having ſomewhat
of the *Play-Houſe* Breeding, is reſolved
not to be wanting in the return of theſe
Civili-

Civilities. She therefore makes him a Glorified Saint for the first piece of Gratitude, and then gives him a sort of Power Paramount to *Omnipotence*, and tells him that God Almighty could not make her happy without him.

I *pray'd* to *thee* as to *a Saint.*
And *thou* hast *heard* my *Prayer,* for *thou*
[*art come* P. 20.
To my Distress, to my Despair; *which Hea-*
[*ven*
Without thee could not Cure.

Almeria has another Flight, and shews the Rankness of her Wing every jot as much as in the former.

'Tis more than Recompence to see thy Face;
If Heaven is greater Joy, it is no Happiness.

This is Mrs. *Brides* Complement, which both for the Religion and Decency is somewhat Extraordinary.

Manuel, a Christian Prince, upon the news of a Rival, Swaggers at a most Impious rate, *Paganism* was never bolder with *Idols,* nor *Jupiter* more brav'd by the Gyants. It runs thus.

[*ven,* Mourn. B.
Better for him to tempt the Rage of Hea- P. 26.
And

And wrench the Bolt red hiffing from the
        [Hand
Of him that Thunders, than but think fuch
        [Infolence,
'Tis daring for a God.

And to make the matter worfe, Mr. *Congreve* does not feem to think this A-

Amend.
P. 30.

theiftical Sally a fault in *Manuel.* He lets us know he has punifh'd him for his Tyranny, but not a word of his Profane-nefs.

Once more and I have done. *Ofmin*'s Careffes of *Almeria* are an Original in their kind.

P. 35.

My all of Blifs, my everlafting Life,
Soul of my Soul, and End of all my Wifhes.

Here's Ceremony to Adoration; He makes her his Supreme Happinefs, and gives her Sovereign Worfhip: In fhort, This Refpect is the Prerogative of Hea-ven. 'Tis flaming Wickednefs to fpeak it to any thing lefs than God Almighty: And to fet the Profanenefs in the better Light, it runs all in devout Language, and Chriftian Tranfport.

I come now to the Vindication of his Poetry: Where in the firft place, he

Amend.
P. 27.

Complains extreamly; becaufe I Mif-quoted *Wafting Air*, for *Wafting Air*.
        Now

Now to my Mind, the restoring of the
Text is a very poor relief. For this later
Epithete is perfectly expletive and foreign
to the matter in hand; there's neither
Antithesis nor Perspicuity in't. It neither
clears the Sense, nor gives Spirit to the
Expression: Besides, the word is almost
worn out of use, and were it otherwise,
'twould rather belong to the *Water*;
For to *waft* a *Fleet* of *Merchants* is to
Convoy them, but not, I suppose, through
the Air: So that the *Poet* at best, seems to
have mistaken his Element. However, I
ask his Pardon for Transcribing an *s*, for
and *f*, and expect he should ask mine;
for putting *Superstition* upon me, and
commenting upon his own Blunder, when
'twas Printed *Supposition* in all the three Amend.
Editions of my Book. P. 44.

Mr. *Congreve* is now Cruizing for Re-
prisals, and bears down boldly upon a
whole *Period*. *This litter of Epithets*, &c. View, &c.
He says *this Comparison* of mine *is handsome*. P. 34.
Why, so it may be for all his Disproof : Amend. p.
Unless the standing of it in his Book is e- 29.
nough to make it ridiculous. I confess
there may be something in that, for bad
Company is often a disadvantage; besides,
I was Illustrating his fine Sentences, and
showing his *Buckram* to the *Reader*: Upon this occasion a little singularity in the

Ex,

Expreſſion was not unſeaſonable : However I was ſenſible of it, and introduced
it with Qualifying, and Caution.

Mr. *Congreve* in defence of ſome Lines
of his Cited by me, Anſwers, that the
Diction of Poetry conſiſts of Figures, and the
frequent uſe of Epithets. I agree with him,
but then the *Figures* ſhould be unforc'd,
drawn with Proportion, and allyed to the
matter in hand. The *Epithets* likewiſe
muſt be Smooth, Natural and Significant.
But when they are lean, and remote from
the buſineſs, when they look hard and
ſtiff, when they clog and incumber the
Senſe, they are no great Ornaments. Whether Mr. *Congreve's* are of this later kind,
or not, I ſhall leave it to the *Reader* to determine !

After a hideous Collection of *Profane-*
neſs, I expreſſed my ſelf with ſomewhat
more than ordinary Concern, as was both
very natural and proper ; Amongſt other
Expreſſions, I ſaid, *Nature made the Fir-*
ment and riſing of the Blood for ſuch Occaſions.
By Nature I grant him, I meant nothing
leſs than God Almighty. That our Me-
chaniſm was contrived ſo as to make our
Paſſions ſerviceable ; Our Conſtitution
adjuſted to our Mind, and our Blood ſo
diſpoſed as to reinforce the operations of
our Reaſon. And pray what is there ex-
cepti-

View, &c.
P. 33, 34.
Amend.
P. 30, 31.

Ariſtotle's
Rhet. L. 3.
C. 2.

ceptionable in all this? And where lies
the Miſtake, in *Religion*, or *natural Philoſophy?* I can hardly forgive my ſelf the
taking notice of ſuch Objections as theſe.
But Mr. *Congreve* was reſolved to make
his *Logick* and *Drollery* of a peice, and I
muſt *be produced* in *Ferment and Figure,*as he
calls it. But this Expreſſion I ſhall leave
with the *Reader*, and give him ſome time
to make Senſe on't. He wonders after
all,why *I ſhould uſe ſo much Vehemence?* Vehemence againſt what? Againſt *Profaneneſs* and *Blaſphemy.* Are theſe then ſuch
harmleſs Practices, that they muſt be
gently treated? Is the Honour of God, the
Intereſt of Religion, and the Welfare of
Humane Society ſo very inſignificant?
Are theſe things beneath our Paſſions, and
not worth the contending for? And won't
they juſtifie a little warmth and expoſtu-
lation in their behalf? *Chriſtianity is Mild,*
'tis true, but not in ſuch caſes as this. The
Cretians did not *Droll* upon their *Bible*
like the Modern *Poets,* and yet St. *Paul*
bids *Titus Rebuke them ſharply.* St. *Peter*
likewiſe and St. *Jude* Laſh the Lewdneſs
of the *Gnoſticks* with great Severity of
Language. But he asks me *why all this
Vehemence in a written Argument?* as if *Paper* would bear Senſe, no more than 'twill
Ink ſometimes, or that People were ob-

*Amend.
P. 34.*

*Tir.1. Pet.
2. 2.
Ibid.*

D 4   liged

liged to write with greater Negligence than they talk. This was a fhrewd queftion! But queftions are eafily ftarted.

Mr. *Congreve* is now come forward to the Vindication of his *Comedys.* He complains that in my Chapter of Profanenefs, Amend. p. 36. I *have reprefented him falfly, or by halves.*

That I have quoted him falfly I deny; neither has he been able to prove it in the leaft Inftance: That he is fometimes reprefented imperfectly I grant. His Immodefty forced me upon this Method. He is often too offenfive to appear. To have fhewn him to the Reader in this Condition, had neither been Civil, nor Safe. Why then does he find fault with this Refervednefs? Is he forry his Indecencies are conceal'd, and grown proud of his Misbehaviour?

We are now with the *Old Batchelour,* and Mr. *Congreve* pretends I'm unfair in not citing *Bellmour* more at length. He fays I conclude *with a dafh, as if both the Senfe and the Words of the whole Sentence were at an end.* Juft the contrary. I made a dafh -------- to fhew there was fomething more fpoken: But though the *Sentence* was not at an end, the *Senfe* was; as appears from the Words, the Pointing, and the *Capital Letter* which follows. Let's fee a little farther, if this Gentleman

has

has received any harm. *Bellmour* is now talking to *Vainlove*.

Bell. *Couldst thou be content to Marry* Araminta ?

Vainlove replies in a very pious questi-on :

Vain. *Could you be content to go to Heaven?*
Bell. *Hum, not immediately in my Con-science, not heartily:* ------ *I'd do a little more good in my generation first in order to deserve it.*

He would do a little more good first, *i. e.* He would gladly be a Libertine some-what longer, and merit Heaven by a more finish'd course of Debauchery. Thus we are taught to interpret *Bellmour* by the *Old Batchelour* and the *Amendments*, &c. He is very lewd in the progress of the *Play*, and Mr. *Congreve* grants, *he re-presents the Character of a wild Debauchee of the Town ; and that the expression is light, and suited accordingly.* Amend. P. 38.

This is a good hearty Confession, and a sufficient proof, that if I had quoted more Words, I had quoted more Pro-faneness ; and therefore Mr. *Congreve* has reason to thank me for being Brief.

Mr.

Mr. *Congreve* drops the Defence of *Fondlewife*, and makes Merry with the Entertainment. His excuse is, he was *very much a Boy when this Comedy was written.* Not unlikely. He and his Muse might probably be Minors; but the Libertines there are full grown. But why should the *Man* laugh at the Mischief of the *Boy*, why should he *publish* the Disorders of his Nonage? and make them his own by an after Approbation? He *wrote it*, it seems, *to amuse himself in a slow Recovery from a Fit of Sickness.* What his Disease was I am not to enquire; but it must be a very ill one, to be worse than the Remedy. The Writing of that Play is a very dangerous Amusement either for *Sickness*, or Health, or I'm much mistaken.

He pleads Guilty to the next Article of Impeachment; but then he is somewhat profane in his very Acknowledgment, and can't find in his heart to give up an old fault, without making a new one.

His next Attempt is to bring off *Bellmour*, who *Kisses* the Strumpet *Lætitia*, and tells her, *Eternity was in that Moment.* Mr. *Congreve*'s Answer is very surprising He tells us, To say *Eternity is in a Moment, is neither good nor bad, for 'tis stark* Nonsense.

By

Ibid p. 39.

Ibid.

p. 40.

P. 40,41.

By his favour, the matter is quite other-wife. If Mr. *Congreve* will have patience, he fhall fpeak Nonfenfe by and by; and to make it the lefs a fault, he fhall do it unwillingly.

Whether this Gentleman borrow'd this Sentence, or made it, I can't tell; but there's juft fuch another in *Love Trium-phant*; where upon fuch an occafion, *Al-* p. 34. *phonfo* tells *Victoria*:

That Moment were Eternity in little.

Now if Mr. *Congreve* has not a mind to fpeak Senfe, I hope Mr. *Dryden* may have leave to do fo. However, we'll prove our Right, and not ftand to his *Courtefie.* Now to fay of an Advan-tage that *Eternity was in that Moment,* is by common Interpretation meant, the Pleafure of Eternity. The Satisfaction is fuppos'd to be fo great, that what is loft in the Duration, is made up in the Quali-ty. This in the prefent Application is hideoufly Profane; but the fenfe and fpi-rit of the Fxpreffion is intelligible enough.

Mr. *Congreve* in the clofe of this Para-gragh is fomewhat extraordinary. He pronounces the Citation *ftark Nonfenfe,* and frankly declares, he *had not cared though I had difcover'd it.* I think I have difcover'd p. 41. it fomewhat worfe. However, I won-

der

der at his being so Resign'd. What not
care to have stark Nonsense found upon
him ; Not in a Printed *Play*, and in the
Mouth of the fine Gentleman ! This is
strange indeed, and I could hardly believe
it at first Sight : But the more I read of
his *Amendments*, &c. the better I am as-
sur'd of the Sincerity of his Confession.

Lætitia has another lewd and very profane Sentence given her, which I had taken notice of. To this Mr. *Congreve*
answers, *'Tis the expression of a wanton and
vicious Character, and that she is discover'd
in her Lewdness.* I reply in the first place,
That my disproof of his second *Postulate*,
or Proposition, cuts off his retreat to this
excuse.

O. Batch.
p. 39.
View, &c.
p. 63.
Amend.
p. 41.

Secondly. She is not discover'd in her
Lewdness, nor makes a dishonourable
Exit ; and Mr. *Congreve* contradicts his
own Play by affirming the contrary. For
there's a Colour found out which passes
upon the Credulity of *Fondlewife*, who
declares himself satisfied with her Innocence. Upon which *Bellmour* concludes
the Fourth Act thus:

O. Batch.
p. 39, 40.

No Husband by his Wife can be deceiv'd,
She still is Virtuous, if she's so believ'd.

Sharper says to *Vainlove*,

I

I have been a kind of Godfather to you yonder,
I have promis'd and vow'd some things in your
Name, which I think you are bound to per-
form. Mr. *Congreve's* answer is. That he Old Batch.
meant no ill by this Allegory, nor perceives any P. 49.
in't now. No *ill in't,* that's Strange! Not Amend.
in applying the solemn Engagements of P. 42.
Baptism to a ridiculous Subject, not in
Burlesquing the *Church Catechism?* If these
are no ill Things, there's no harm in Profaneness ; and then I confess he has justified himself to purpose.

Before we part with the *Old Batchelour,* O. Batch.
I'll give Mr. *Congreve* another Citation P. 48.
unmention'd before.

Heartwell speaking of Marriage, cries
out, *O cursed State !*
    How wide we err
    When apprehensive of the Load of Life
    ------ *We hope to find*
That help which Nature meant in Womankind

It seems then Nature was as much mistaken in the provision, as Men are in the
Experiment. Yes, for as the Poet goes
on :

And Adam *sure wou'd with more ease abide* Ib. p. 48.
The Bone when broken, than when made a Bride.

This is an admirable Comment on the
Old

Old and New Testament, and the Office
of Matrimony in the Common Prayer.
The Thought looks like an Improvement
of a Line in *Abſalom* and *Achitophel* : where
the ſubjeƈt of the Poem is dated from the
times of *Polygamy*,

Abſal. &
Achit. p. 1.
    E're one to one was curſedly Confined.

    The *Provoked Wife* has a Sentence not
much ſhort of this.

p. 27.
    Sure (ſays Sir *John Brute*) *If Woman
had been ready Created, the Devil inſtead of
being kicked down into Hell, had been Married.*

    We are now with the *Double Dealer* ;
View, &c.
p. 64.
where, as I remark'd, Lady *Plyant* cries
out *Jeſu*, and *talks Smut in the ſame Sentence.* Here again he pleads Guilty :
He *had condemn'd it long ſince, and reſolved*
Amend.
P. 42.
to ſtrike it out in the next Impreſſion. Well!
Repentance is a very commendable thing,
and I heartily wiſh Mr. *Congreve* may go
Through with it. But I'm afraid this
good Reſolution of his went off in a little
time : My reaſon is, becauſe the *Double
Dealer* was publiſh'd in 1694. and ſtands
ſtill in the Firſt *Edition* ; But the *Old Batchelour* has been Reprinted long ſince, the
Sixth Impreſſion of this Play bearing date
1697.

1697. And yet here in this laſt Edition we have the exclamation *Jeſu*, uſed in a jeſting way, by the fulſome *Belinda*. If Mr. ^{Old Batch.} *Congreve* was diſpleas'd with the Profane- ^{p. 48.} neſs in his *Double Dealer*, why did he not expunge it in his *Old Batchelour*? He can't deny but that Opportunity preſented fair a great while together. But here inſtead of asking Pardon of God and the World, and ſhewing himſelf concern'd for ſo ſcandalous an Expreſſion, He tells you a pleaſant Story (as he fancies) of a Letter of Advice from an *Old Gentlewoman, and a Widow, who as ſhe ſaid, was very well to paſs.* I ſuppoſe ſhe ſubſcrib'd her ſelf Old Gentlewoman, as Widows generally do, otherwiſe, as far as appears, he had been at a loſs for her Age. But to return. Either this Story is pretended or real. If 'tis a feigned caſe, 'tis nothing to his point. If 'tis matter of Fact, it makes againſt him. For then he makes a Jeſt of his own Reformation, Drolls upon *good Counſel*, and returns the Gentlewoman an Affront in Publick, for her Charitable Admonitions in Private. As for the *Smut*, he tells me, if there is any, *I may e'en take it for my pains.* ^{Amend.} Very generouſly argued! Since he is thus ^{p. 43.} Noble, I'le omit the Scrutiny, and only refer to the Page.

^{Double D.}
^{p. 34.}

And

And here the Reader may pleafe to take notice, that the word *Jefu* is thrice made bold with, in defpight of Religion and the Statute 3 *Jac.* 1. *cap.* 21.

D. Dealer.
p.7,16,78.

Sir *Paul Plyant* among the reft of his Follies, is mighty fond of the word *Providence*, and repeats it on feveral occafions. From hence I drew this natural, or rather neceffary Inference; That the meaning was to fhew, that Senfe and Religion agreed ill together, and that none but Fools were fit to talk pioufly. Mr. *Congreve* inftead of defending himfelf, endeavours to make me fpeak Nonfenfe, but that lies all in his own mifquotation; as I have fhewn already.

He pretends there's no profane Allufion in his little Drollery about *Jehu*'s *being a Hackney Coachman*; And feems confident no other *Text* can be burlefqu'd excepting *Lady Froth*'s *Poem.* He fays Lady *Froth* calls the *Coachman our* Jehu, *and why might he not have that as well as any Jewifh or Chriftian Name?* I'le tell him for once. 'Twas never the Cuftom of Jews or Chriftians to take any *Scripture* Names from exceptionable Perfons. Neither *Jeroboam* nor *Jehu*, nor many others, were Religious enough for this purpofe. No Man I believe ever heard of more than two *Jehu*'s, one in the *Kings*, and the other in the

Amend.
P. 44,45.

2 Kings 9.
20.

Double

Double Dealer. That Prince in the *King's is said to drive his Chariot furiously.* From hence the *Coachman's* Character was Equip'd. Both the Name and the Office, have a plain reference to the Holy Text. Farther, *Lady Froth* does not call her Coachman by any Name in her Poem; by consequence the Afterism for direction, can never lead us to the meaning of her Verses. For if *Jehu* is unmention'd in the Poetick Text, how can the Lady be explain'd by his Standing in the Margin? In short, the worthy Mystery can't be clear'd up without recourse to the *Scriptures*; And therefore without doubt we are much obliged to the Poet for this necessity. Thus 'tis plain the Bible is made Bold with, and the Turn of his expression seems to reach the *Commentators* too. However, if his meaning is over-strain'd on this later particular, it will do him very little Service; and I ask his excuse. I'm sorry to spend so many words about such Stuff as this is; but Mr. *Congreve* must have Justice done him.

Sir *Paul Plyant* will afford us something worse than the former; This *Wittoll* of the Poet's making, tells his Lady he finds Passion *coming upon him by Inspiration.* This I had reason to Charge upon Mr. *Congreve* as a very profane Expression:

E   In

In answer to this, He first Rails a Sentence or two in his little way, and then very Magisterially tells us, *That the word Inspiration, when it has Divine prefix'd to it, bears a particular and known signification: But otherwise to inspire is no more than to Breath into; and a Trumpet, &c. may be said without profaneness to deliver a Musical Sound by the help of Inspiration.* By his favour, All People that talk *English* know, that Inspiration, when it stands without Epithets and Addition, is always taken in a Religious signification. Inspiration, and to be Inspired, have a solemn and august meaning in Christianity. These words imply Divine Impulse, and supernatural Assistance, and are oppos'd to suggestion of Fancy, and humane Reasoning. To speak by Inspiration is to speak by the *Holy Ghost,* as every Body can tell him: To be *saved* and *Salvation,* signified at first no more than Safety, and Escape: But if a Man should say, *As he hop'd to saved,* and explain himself, that he intended no more, then that he hoped to get Cover before a Shower reach'd him; would he not be look'd upon as impertinently profane? If he call'd a lucky Leap of a Ditch *Salvation,* and pretended to justifie himself, that the word originally imports no more than Common

De-

Deliverance, what Place would he be
thought fit for? Thus when Words are
made Inclofure, when they are reftrain'd
by Common Ufage, and tyed up to a
particular Senfe : In this Cafe, to run up
to Etymology, and Conftrue them by
Dictionary and *Præpofition*, is wretchedly
Ridiculous and Pedantick. *Horace* can
tell him, That Cuftom over-rules *Syllables*,
and gives Law to Language.

De Art.
Poet.

Quem penes arbitrium eſt, & jus & norma
*   loquendi.*

Mr. *Congreve* perceiving himfelf prefs'd
retires with all Speed to his Fourth Pro-
pofition. But that I have difabled already.
If he is poifon'd with his Profanenefs, and
finds himfelf Sick, he muft take what
follows; for his Antidote is gone. To
return to Sir *Paul.*

I find Paſſion (fays he) *coming upon*
me by Infpiration, and I cannot fubmit as
formerly.

D. *D*.*ale*
P. 1).

You fee what an admirable reafon he
urges in Defence of his Folly, from the
extraordinary Circumftances of it ! No
Prophet could have juftified his Refent-
ments from a higher pretence.

E 2   The

The fine Lady *Cynthia* out of her pious Education acquaints us, That *though Marriage makes Man and Wife one Flesh, it leaves them still two Fools.* But the little word STILL is left out in the Quotation; which like the Fly on the *Coach-Wheel*, raises a mighty Dust. I grant I have by Chance omitted the word STILL; and if he had done so too, the Sense had been perfectly the same, only better expressed. For *Still* is plainly useless, and comprehended in the Verb *Leaves.* For if *Marriage leaves 'em two Fools*, they are Fools after Marriage, and then they are Fools *Still*, I think; Nothing can be clearer than this. But besides, *Cynthia* her self won't allow of Mr. *Congreve's* excuse. For after she has deliver'd that remarkable Sentence of *leaving 'em two Fools*, &c. *Mellifont* answers, *That's only when two Fools meet*, which is exactly Mr. *Congreve* in his *Amendments.* This *Cynthia* denies to be her meaning. *Cynth. Nay* (says she) *I have known two Wits meet, and by the opposition of their Wits render themselves as ridiculous as Fools.* And therefore after she has given Matrimony an odd Name, she advises him to Court no farther, to *draw Stakes, and give over in time.* So that besides Burlesquing the Bible, the Satyr is pointed against Marriage. And the

Folly

P. 47.

D. Dealer.
P. 18.

Folly is made to lye in the State, as well
as in the Perfons. Upon the whole, we
fee the *Double Dealer*, and the *Amendments*
can't agree; and thus two Blemifhes, as
well as two Beauties, are fometimes unlike to each other. Mr. *Congreve* fays,
*Ben. Johnfon is much bolder in the firft Scene
of his Bartholomew Fair.* Suppofe all that.
Is it an excufe to follow an ill Example,
and continue an Atheiftical practice ? I
thought Mr. *Congreve in his penetration*
might have feen through this Queftion.
Ben. Johnfon (as he goes on) *makes Littlewit fay, Man and Wife make one Fool. I
have faid nothing comparable to that.* No- Amend. P. 47.
thing comparable! Truly in the ufual
fenfe of that Phrafe, Mr. *Congreve*, 'tis
poffible, has faid nothing comparable to
Ben. Johnfon, nor it may be never will :
But in his new Propriety he has faid fomething more than comparable, that is a
great deal worfe. For though *Littlewit*'s
Allufion is profane, the words of the *Bible* are fpared. He does not Droll directly
upon *Genefis*, or St. *Matthew* ; Upon God
the Son, or God the Holy Ghoft : Whereas Mr. *Congreve* has done that which
amounts to both. And fince he endeavours to excufe himfelf upon the Authority of *Ben. Johnfon*, I fhall juft mention
what Thoughts this Poet had of his pro-

fane

fane Liberties, at a time when we have reafon to believe him moſt in earneſt. Now Mr. *Wood* reports from the Teſtimony of a great Prelate then preſent.

Athen.
Oxonienſ.
Vol. 1.
P. 519. " That when *Ben. Johnſon* was in his laſt " Sickneſs, he was often heard to repent " of his profaning the Scriptures in his " Plays, and that with Horrour.

Now as far as I can perceive, the Smut and Profaneneſs of Mr. *Congreve*'s Four Plays out-ſwell the Bulk of *Ben. Johnſon*'s Folio. I heartily wiſh this Relation may be ſerviceable to Mr. *Congreve*, and that as his Faults are greater, his Repentance may come ſooner.

S. Ambro. *Quem ſecutus es peccantem, ſequere pœnitentem.*

The *Double Dealer* is now done with, and Mr. *Congreve* concludes his Vindication in his uſual Strain of Triumph and Aſſurance.

Love for Love comes at laſt upon the Board. In this *Play* I blamed him for making a *Martyr* of a Whoremaſter: Upon this, he flies immediately for Succour to *Scapula*, and the *Greek Grammar*. He very learnedly tells us, that Martyr is a Greek *word, and ſignifies in plain Engliſh no more than a Witneſſ.* Right! theſe two words are the ſame ; and when a

Cauſe

Caufe comes on in *Weftminfter-Hall*, the *Martyrs* are call'd immediately! But *Martyr* is but bare *Witnefs* in the Greek. Not always: Chriftian Writers often ufe it in a fenfe appropriated. And were it otherwife, there's no arguing from one Language to another. *Tyrant* was once an Honourable Name in *Greek*, but always a Reproach in *Englifh*. But to dilate upon thefe Cavils, is throwing away time. If the Reader defires more, he may pleafe to look back on my Anfwer to his Objection about *Infpiration*.

This *Poet's* way of underftanding *Englifh*, puts me in mind of a late Misfortune which happen'd to a Country Apothecary. The Dr. had prefcrib'd a Lady Phyfick to be taken in fomething Liquid, which the Bill according to Cuftom call'd a *Vehicle*. The Apothecary being at a Stand about the word, applies, as Mr. *Congreve* might have done, to *Littleton's Dictionary*. And there he finds *Vehiculum* fignified feveral confiderable Things. He makes up the *Bill*, and away he goes to the Lady, where upon the Queftion, how the Phyfick was to be taken? He anfwers very innocently; Madam, fays he, You may take it in a *Cart*, or a *Waggon*, but not to give your Ladyfhip too much trouble, I think a *Wheelbarrow* may

do;

do; for the word *Vehicle* in the Bill, will carry that sense. In short, This Direction was comply'd with, and the *Footman* drove the *Wheelbarrow* about the Chamber. To return to Mr. *Congreve.* I had said that this Libertine Application of his, was dignifying Adultery with the Stile of

Ibid. Martyrdom; As if (says Mr. *Congreve*) *any word could dignifie Vice.* And pray why not? Does not the Varnish hide the Coarseness underneath, and the Pill go down the better for the Guilding? Whether he knows it or not, there's a great deal of Charm and Imposture in *Words*; and an ill practice is often comply'd with upon the Strength of a Fashionable Name.

He asks, who told me Jeremy Fetch *was* P. 49. *bred at the University?* Why *Jeremy* says so himself pretty plainly, and *Tattle* says so, and I suppose Mr. *Congreve* says as much as that comes to in his Reflection immedi-

Love for L. ately following. But this notable questi-
P. 75. on was put to introduce another Business
Amend.
P. 50. of greater Consequence. For upon this occasion, out of *his excellence* of *good Manners,* he is pleased to observe, That *I should not have been suspected of an University Education any more than his* Jeremy *in the Play, if I had not Printed* M. A. *on the Title Page.* Here the Poor Man has shewn his Will, and his Weakness sufficiently!

I'm

I'm almoſt ſorry 'tis ſo low with him.
When a Poet is ſo extreamly well inclin'd
to be Witty, 'tis pity he has no more in
his power. Mr. *Congreve* goes on Man-
fully in his Defence and ſays, *For the word* Amend.
Whoreſon, I had it from Shakeſpear *and* p. 50.
Johnſon. Not unlikely. People are apt
to learn what they ſhould not. Mr. *Con-*
greve's Memory, or his Invention, is very
conſiderable this way. Indeed one would
almoſt think by his Writings, that he had
digeſted ill Language into a Common
Place. But it was not only *Whoreſon,*
but *Jeremy's* ſaying He was Born with
Whoreſon Appetites, which I complain'd
of ; and which I take to be Blaſpheming
the Creation.

He pretends I have vvrong'd him
ſtrangely in a Rant of Sir *Sampſon's* : And
would make the Reader believe I charge
him literally with Paraphraſing the 139*th* Amend.
Pſalm. I'm ſorry I'm forced to explain p. 51.
my ſelf in ſo clear a caſe.

We may obſerve then, that the Pſal-
miſt in Contemplation of the aſtoniſhing
Beauty and Serviceableneſs of Humane
Bodies, breaks out in a Rapture of Gra-
titude, *I will give thanks unto thee, for I* Pſal. 139.
am fearfully and wonderfully made, marvel- v. 13.
lous are thy works, and that my Soul knows
right well. Let us now hear Sir *Sampſon.*

This

This Gentleman after having railed a Lecture over *Jeremy*'s Body, for being born with Necessities too big for his Condition; he crys, *These things are unacountable, and unreasonable*; *Why was not I a Bear?* --- *Nature has been provident only to Bears and Spiders* : Thus we see what a Harmony of Thought there is between *David* and our Author. The one Adores while the other Reproaches. The one Admires, the other Burlesques the wonders of Providence. And this was all the *Paraphrasing* I meant, as any one might easily Imagine.

Love for L.
P. 25.

The Dialogue of *Scandal* and *Foresight* lies next in our way, I shall once more Transcribe it from *Love for Love.*

P. 44.

Fore. Alas Mr. *Scandal,* Humanum est errare.

Scand. You say true, Man *will err*; *meer* Man *will err* ---- *but you are something more* --- *There have been wise Men, but they were such as you ---- Men who consulted the Stars, and were observers of Omens* --- Solomon *was wise, but how? By his Judgment in Astrology,* ----- So *says Pineda* in his Third Book and eighth Chap. But (says Mr. *Congreve*) the *Quotation* of the *Authority* is *omitted* by Mr. Collier, *either because he would* represent *it as my own Observation to ridicule the Wisdom* of Solomon *or else because he*

was

was indeed Ignorant that it belong'd to any bo- Amend.
dy else. To this I answer, p. 52.

1. That Mr. *Congreve* yields *Solomon*'s Wisdom ridiculed by *this Observation*, therefore by his own confession, if 'tis none of his Authors, he must Answer for't himself. Now *Pineda* gives us a quite different account of the Cause of *Solomon*'s Wisdom, and which is perfectly inconsistent with *Congreve*'s Banter. " *Pineda* af-
" firms that *Solomon*'s Wisdom was given
" him by God in a supernatural Dream, 1. Kings 3.
" mentioned in Scripture. And that after 5, 12.
" the Dream, he found an unusual Light Pined.Lib.
" in his Understanding; his Ideas were 3. Cap. 8.
" brighten'd, and the extent of his Know- P. 142,
" ledge strangly enlarged. 'Tis true, *Pi-* 147.
" *neda* believed that *Solomon* understood Ed. Mo-
gunt.
" *Astronomy* in Perfection, and that he had Lib. 3. C.
" skill in *Prognosticks* which he calls *A-* 18.
" *stronomia judiciaria.* He continues, that
" he could in a great measure reach the In-
" clinations and Reasonings of Men, where
" they did not depend purely upon choice, Ibid.
" and the turn of the *Will.* But then he
" does not say that *Solomon*'s Skill in *Prog-*
" *nosticks* was that which made him *wise.*
" No: This Tallent was only a Branch,
" but not the Cause of his Wisdom. For
" as *Pineda* speaks elsewhere, *Solomon* had Lib. 3 C.
" a Universal Knowledge of Nature, but 10.
" then

" then this Excellency was no result of
" Natural parts, or Humane Industry;
" 'Twas an immediate Bounty from Hea-
" ven; And both the Thing, and the Con-
" veyance, were extraordinary.

Mr. *Congreve* agrees with *Pineda* at
least in a jesting way, *Solomon* was *wise,
but how? By his Judgment in Astrology.*
That is, his distinguishing Attainments
were gained this way. There was nothing
in the case, but that he had looked into a
Star somewhat farther than other people :
He Learned his Wisdom it seems from
the *Caldeans,* or *Ægyptians,* or from some
such Book as *Lillies Almanack.* This is
Scandal's Solution of the Mystery ; and the
best that I can make on it. For t'is one
thing to say that a Man is *wise* by *Astrology,* and another that *Astrology* or *Astronomy* was only a part of his Wisdom. The
one Implies the Cause, and the other but
a Branch of the Effect. The one excludes
the Miracle, and the other affirms it.
Upon the whole matter, Mr. *Congreve,*
and *Pineda,* are not to be reconciled, so
that by his own confession he has *ridiculed
the Wisdom of Solomon,* and falsifyed his
Author into the Bargain.

2*ly.* Supposing *Pineda* had been fairly
reported by Mr. *Congreve,* the *Poet* had
been much to blame ; For then the Case
had

had stood thus; *Pineda* as Mr. *Congreve* observes had ridiculed *Solomon*, and himself had done no less, by Citing him without Censure, and upon a Drolling Occasion. For this reason I waved the consulting of *Pineda*, as well knowing that should the Testimony have been right, the *Play* was certainly in the wrong. Besides, 'tis somewhat to be suspected Mr. *Congreve* never saw *Pineda*; My reason is, because he falls twice into the same Mistake, he Quotes the *Eighteenth* Chapter for the *Eighth*, and to make it appear the more gross, 'tis done in words of Length, and not in Figures. I hope for the future Mr. *Congreve* wont bring in *Solomon* to divert the *Play-House*, nor compare him with Fools and Fortunetellers. Lov. for L. P. 44. Amend. P. 52.

Scandal's telling *Foresight* he was *more than meer Man*, and secure from Mistake upon that Score, is likewise a profane expression. To affirm this of any person, is as much as to say, he is either our *Saviour*, or a *Prophet*, or under some Miraculous Influence.

Scandal goes on with *Foresight*, " and " sayes the Wise Men of the East ow'd " their Instruction to a Star, which is " rightly observed by *Gregory* the Great " in favour of *Astrology*. Lov. for L. P. 44.

Mr. *Con-*

Mr. *Congreve* vindicates this paſſage by ſaying, that *Scandal Banters Foreſight,* but *not the Audience.* Not Banter the Audience! He Affronts the Audience I'm ſure, if they have any Chriſtianity in them, by drolling upon a Miracle at our Saviour's Birth: He banters St. *Matthew* too, who has recorded the Miracle, and *Gregory* the Great, who diſcourſes upon it.

Mr. *Congreve* is pleaſed to ſay that *I am very angry that Sir Sampſon has not another Name,* becauſe *Sampſon is a Name in the Old Teſtament.* This is falſe in every ſyllable, as the Reader may ſee by conſulting my Book. But this I ſay, that Mr. *Congreve* has burleſqu'd the Hiſtory of *Sampſon,* and wreſted the *Scripture* into Smut.

Amend. 54.
Judges 16. 30.
Love for Love, p. 74. Ed. 3<i>d</i>.</div>

There are two other profane Paſſages Cenſur'd by me in the ſame Page: Theſe he leaves as it were to ſhift for themſelves, and has not as yet, made them worſe by defending them: Excepting that he comes up with his old Cavil about the Word *Martyr,* which I have anſwer'd already.

The next Place Mr. *Congreve* leads us to is *Bedlam:* And here he gives us three Reaſons for *Valentine's* pretended Madneſs. The two later are ſomewhat extraordinary. He makes him Mad it ſeems

for

for a variation of the Character. A shrewd Amend. P. 55.
Contrivance, to put a Man out of his
Wits for the sake of Variety? For without doubt, Raving and Incoherence are
wonderfully taking. I suppose Mr. *Con-* Amend. P. 41.
greve made *Bellmour* talk Nonsense for this
wise reason. For 'tis a dull thing for a
Man to be always tyed up to Sense, and
confin'd to his Understanding. His third Amend. p. 56.
reason for taking away Reason, is *because*
Madness gives a liberty to Satyr, and autho-
rises a Bluntness, &c. which would otherwise
have been a Breach of Manners in the Cha-
racter. That is, it gives *Valentine* a Commission to talk Smut, and abuse his Fa-
ther. But Mr. *Congreve* needed not to Love for Love, p. 57, 58, 63.
have given himself this trouble about *Va-*
lentine ; For *Valentine* when he was in his
Wits, and under the Character of a fine
Gentleman, had Breeding enough to be Love for L. p. 7. 23, 24, 83. Ed. 3d.
Smutty, and Undutiful. Mr. *Congreve*
would perswade the Reader that I interpret him with too much Rigour, for making *Valentine* in his Lunacy say, *I am*
Truth, &c. If this Point needs any farther
Disputing, we may take notice that our
Blessed Saviour mentions the word *Truth* Joh. 14.6. 17. viii. 32 xvii. 17, 18 xviii. 18, 31.
in a solemn and peculiar manner. He
sometimes applies it to Himself, sometimes to the Holy Ghost, and sometimes
to the Revelation of the Gospel. In short,

'tis

'tis as it were appropriated to the greateſt Perſons, and Things, mark'd as the Prerogative of God ; and uſed in a ſenſe of Emphaſis and Diſtinction. Let us compare St. *John*, and Mr. *Congreve* a little, and then we may eaſily judge where the Fault lies.

St. *Thomas* anſwers our Bleſſed Saviour, *Lord we know now not whither thou go-*Joh.14.6. *eſt, and how can we know the way? Jeſus ſaith unto him, I am the Way ,and the Truth, and the Life.* Sir *Sampſon* is at a loſs, Swears, and cries out, *I know not which* Love forL *way to go.* Valentine enquires, *Who's that,* p.57. Ed.3 *that's out of his Way? I am Truth, and can ſet him right.*

Our Saviour aſſures his Diſciples, That he will ſend them the *Comforter*. And Joh. 16.13 that *when he the Spirit of Truth is come, he will guide you into all Truth, and he will ſhew you things to come.*

The execrable *Valentine* ſays, *Interrupt me not --- I'll whiſper Prediction to thee, and* P. 62. 55. *thou ſhalt Propheſie. I am Truth, and can* L. for Lo. *teach thy Tongue a new Trick : I am Truth,* 2d. & 3d. *and come to give the World the Lie.*

And is not this horrible Stuff ? What can be more intolerable Boldneſs, than thus to uſurp the Regal Sitile, to proſtitute the Language of Heaven, and apply it to Drollery and Diſtraction ?

Mr.

Mr. *Congreve* is advanced to my 3 *d* Chapter, concerning the Abuſe of the Clergy. As for the Diſſenting *Miniſters*, he ſays I charge him with nothing more than *Setter's*, procuring their Habit for *Bellmour*. Under favour, this is a great Miſtake. The Pimp reads a Lecture of Abuſe upon the Habit, expoſes *Spintext* from Head to Foot, makes him both a Knave and a Libertine, and his Wife a Whore into the bargain. The *View*, &c. has remark'd, *that Barnaby calls another of that Character Mr. Prig.* He does ſo. And *Fondlewife* repreſents him lewd in a luſcious Deſcription. Mr. *Congreve* replies, *What if his Name were Mr.* Prig, *or what if it were not?* Now 'tis poſſible he'll not like it, if I don't conſider theſe weighty Queſtions. I ſay then, If his Name was ſo, he has misbehaved himſelf by putting him in his *Play*. If 'twere not ſo, He has uſed the Diſſenting Miniſters ill, by repreſenting one of their Order in a contemptuous Manner. For as he himſelf confeſſes, a Mr. *Prig*, and a Mr. *Smirk*, *are Names implying Characters worthy of Averſion and Contempt.* Now for a Man not to underſtand his own ill Language , and contradict himſelf in a few Pages, is, in his own decent expreſſion, *furiouſly ſimple.*

Mr. *Congreve* pretends that a Reflection on a *Lord's Chaplain* is no Reflection on a

Amend. p. 57.

View, &c. p. 102.
Old Batch. p. 19, 20.

View, &c. p. 102.

Amend. P. 58.

Amend. p. 76.

Amend. p. 58.
See O. Bat. p. 27.

Parſon

Parson of the Church of *England*. That's
somewhat strange. The *Roman* Catholick
Lords have no *Chaplains*; the Law does not
allow it. And as for the Dissenters, there
are very few Lords of their Perswasion. I
desire therefore to know upon what Party
the Abuse must stick? In earnest, I'm almost
tired with answering these things. To
strike the Air, does but make a Man's Arm
ake.

There is a pretty long Instance produced
from the *Double Dealer*, to shew the Misbehaviour of the *Stage* towards the Clergy;
these Passages he leaves to take their Fortune; for they have nothing in them it
P. 59. seems, which *needs a Defence*. This is a dis-
creet way of answering; and I think, if he
had made more use on't, it might have done
as well.

To shew the Unreasonableness of the
Stage in representing the Clergy under Characters of Disadvantage and Contempt, I
endeavour'd to vindicate the Reputation of
that *Order* from three Topicks.

1*st*. From their Relation to the Deity.

2*ly*. From the Importance of their Office.

3*ly*. Because they had general Custom,
and Prescription for their Privilege.

Under the First Head, I had said that the
View, *&c.* *Credit of the Service always rises in Proportion*
P. 127. *to the Quality and Greatness of the Master.*
This

This Position, he says, is *sophistical*; and yet he is so Civil as to grant it in the next Line Amend. P. 61. but one. However, he makes a Stand at the Inference, and asserts, That *though the* Ibid. *Credit of the Service rises in proportion to the Quality of the Master, yet the Credit of the Servant, does not rise in proportion to the Credit of the Service.* Not rise in proportion to the Credit of the Service; that's strange! I thought Office and Authority had been a just ground for Regard; and that Honourable Charges had made Honourable Men. And if so, I suppose the Esteem of the Person must improve with the Credit of the Employment. I would gladly know in what Circumstance the Dignity of an Ambassador consists? Does it not lye in his Commission and Credentials, in the Advantage and Significancy of his Character? What makes such a Person treated with greater Regard, than a *Factor*, or private *Agent*? Is it not the Honour of the Representation, and the Weight of the Business? Now he that executes for another, or represents him by way of Authority, is without doubt in his Service: From whence it follows, That if the Credit of the *Servant* rises by the Quality of the Business, and Authority, it must by consequence rise in proportion to the Credit of the Service; for these are only different words to signify the

same

Amend.
p 61.

same thing : Mr. *Congreve*'s saying, That *an ill Servant both discredits his Service, and is discredited by it* ; is partly foreign, and partly false. To say he is discredited by it, is untrue. For 'tis the Misbehaviour, not the Office, which gives the Discredit. And then to say that an *ill Servant discredits his Service*, is nothing to his point. For the purpose. Suppose the Ministers of *State* or *Justice*, in any Government, should fail in their Conduct: Are they presently to be insulted by the Common People, exposed in the Badges of their Character, and made the Diversion of the Town? What if a Man is an ill Servant, his Commission ought to be his protection from private Indignities. As for his Mismanaging, he must account to his Master; Equals or Inferiours, have nothing to do to punish. Mr. *Congreve* adds, that *if a Servant is punish'd by the Law, the Honour of the Service is not by that means violated.* As much Law as he pleases; Let Justice have its Course, and I'm contented. But what's this to the Stage? Have they a Patent of Jurisdiction over the Clergy? Are they authorised to pronounce upon their Faults, and their Punishment? To give them little Behaviour, and contemptuous Usage; To make them Fools, and then treat them as such?

Amend.
p. 62.

But now 'tis Mr. *Congreve*'s turn to ask Queſtions : He would know of me, *Whe-* Amend. *ther a Man after he has received Holy Orders,* p. 53. *is become incapable of either playing the Knave or the Fool?* Why truly, conſidering he has the ſame Humane Nature with a Poet, I can't think him utterly incapable of either. And now I may have anſwer'd his queſtion as civilly as he ask'd it.

But if a Clergy-man plays the Fool, he is Ibid. *equally with a Lay-Fool, the ſubject of Laughter and Contempt.* Not in the ſame way neither. Circumſtances alter any Caſe. Different Things require different Conſiderations. There are Laws, Diſcipline, and *Ordinaries,* to take care of greater Miſcarriages in the Church. And as for leſſer Misfortunes, they ſhould rather be lamented, than expos'd. The Clergy are a ſort of Spiritual Parents. St. *Paul*'s reaſoning ſuppoſes it : And the Church Catechiſm gives them an inference of Privilege from the Fifth Commandment. To banter a Relation of this kind, has neither Decency, nor Religion in't. And we know *Ham* got no Bleſſing by his Diſcovery. To ſtigmatize a ſolemn Character, to play the Buffoon in a Gown and Caſſock, and ſhew the Church for a *Monſter,* is, one would think, an odd diverſion in Chriſtendom. The Heathens treated the Primitive Chriſtians much at this rate :

They

They wrapt them in Bear-skins, and then set the Dogs on them.

But Mr. *Congreve* urges, That by improper *Behaviour the Man becomes alienated from the Prieſt, and ſo the Folly is expoſed, not the Function.* For example, if the Man be knock'd on the Head, the Prieſt is not a jot the worſe for't. This is much like the old Diſtinction of *Politick*, and *Perſonal Capacity*, applied to another Caſe. To give this Gentleman an Anſwer more at large, he may pleaſe to take notice:

Ibid.

1*ſt.* Though the Function and the Perſon are ſeparable in Notion, they are joyn'd in Life and Buſineſs. 'Tis true, the Office and the Perſon are two Things ; but yet 'tis the Perſon which executes the Office : This makes them ſhare a diſadvantage in Common ; and a Cenſure frequently ſlides from the one to the other. If you make the Man a Knave, the Prieſt muſt ſuffer under the Imputation : And a Fool in his *Perſon*, will never be thought diſcreet in his Function. Upon this account Perſons in Authority, whether Spiritual or Civil, ought to be privileg'd from Abuſe. To make the Miniſters of *Church* or *State*, the *ſubject of Laughter and Contempt*, diſables their Authority, and renders their Commiſſion inſignificant. The Heathen Dramatiſts ſeem ſenſible of this reaſoning, and practiſe accordingly.

See View, p. 122.

2*ly.* If

2*ly.*If the Poets defign was no more than to *expofe and reprehend Folly and Vice in general,* why are not the Failings of the Clergy reprefented in a Lay-Appearance ? Why muft the Satyr be pointed at the *Coat,* and run out into Reference and Diftinction? Why muft the Profeffion be dreffed up, and the Folly keep all within the Function ? Is not this plainly to confound the Order and the Mifcarriage, to go off from the *Man* to the *Prieft,* and render them both ridiculous?

3*ly.* Employments are oftentimes a fhelter to Perfons; and Characters a Protection from Infult: Publick Reafon will not endure Authority to be expos'd, or the Magiftrates to be made a *May-Game.* To talk in Mr.*Congreve's* Language, a *Lay-Fool* is not always to be faluted by his Folly. This would be great rudenefs in Converfation ; and the Government might fuffer by it. Condition is a Cover for Failings. And Authority muft not be a Jeft. In this cafe a Man fhould be view'd on the fide of Advantage, and treated by his beft Diftinction. Now if we confider the Author, and the Ends of Church Authority, we fhall find it deferves a Guard, no lefs than that of the *State.*

The Church-Article quoted by Mr. *Congreve,* does him no Service. If it has any reference to the matter in hand, it makes

againft

against him. The Article affirms, That
*Evil Ministers Act by Christ's Authority and
Commission*; That the *Word and Sacraments
are significant and effectual in their Hands*;
and that the Indisposition of the *Agent*, does
not weaken the *Institution.* Now since
even a vicious Priest represents our Saviour,
since he is God's Ambassadour, and is a Conveyance of the Blessings of Heaven: These
Credentials, these Benefits, one would
think, might guard him from Contempt,
and make his Character inviolable. 'Tis
true, the Article says, They *may be accus'd,
and being found guilty, by just Judgment de-
pos'd.* But what of all this? Are the *Poets*
their Judges? And is the Stage grown *Do-
ctors Commons*, or *Westminster-Hall*? Well:
But the Article supposes a *Distinction between
the Man, and the Priest.* Yes: And it supposes too, that the Man ought to fare the
better for this double Capacity. Mr. *Congreve* in citing this Quotation, has mistaken
the Chronology, and confounded the *Arti-
cles* and *Canons*, but this I shall pass over.

But Mr. *Congreve* falls into a worse Mistake than the former. He makes St. *Cyprian*
affirm that the Validity of the *Sacraments*
depends on the Probity of the Priest, and
that the Article was partly *established to take
off the Authority of this Father.*

Amend.
p. 67.

Amend.
p. 64.

Ib. p 66.

Now

Now to say this, is to misreport St. *Cyprian*. 'Tis true, this worthy Prelate believed that a Priests Authority was suspended by *Heresy* and *Schism*; but that bare Immorality could recall his Commission, he does no where suppose. The Case of *Basilides* and *Martialis*, if Mr. *Congreve* had produced it, would not come up to the Point: For this Instance concerns Sacrificing to Idols; which is an Act of Apostacy: It implies a renouncing of Christianity. From whence it will follow, that those who are not so much as Members of the Church, cannot have the Power of Church-Governours.

Mr. *Congreve* seems displeas'd with that little Justice I endeavoured to do the Clergy; And calls the Testimonies of the best *Poets, Orators, Historians,* &c. *Vain Stuff.* P. 71. *I take it (* says Mr. *Congreve) he would give us to understand, that in all Ages the Function of a Priest was held to be a very Honourable Function; Did Mr.* Collier *ever meet with any body Fool enough to engage him to assert that?* Ibid. Many a one, I can assure you, that have been either Fool or Knave enough, I can't tell which. If the Post is Honourable, the Persons should be considered accordingly: They should not be exposed in a wretched Appearance; And have neither Sense nor Spirit, nor fair usage allowed them.

See View, &c. Ch. 3. them. The *Heathen Poets*, as I prov'd at large, never serv'd their Priests so.

Amend. P. 71. 72. Mr. *Congreve* urges, that *Kings have been in all Ages Exposed and Punish'd on the Stage, yet never any King complained of the* Theater *or the* Poets. From hence he argues, that if *Kings may be exposed on the Stage* ; Why not Priests ? To this I answer,

1*st*. Mr. *Congreve*'s Argument supposes that *Poets* have the leave of *Princes* for this Freedom. Kings it seems are willing to be brought, and Disciplined on the Stage. Very well. But does the *Hierarchy* desire to be represented ? Does the Church give the *Play-House* this Permission ? By no means. She Complains of the Practice, and would have it otherwise. Now what Consequence is there from Permission to Remonstrance, and from Pleasure to Aversion ? The Church does not desire to be so Publick. Why should she be hal'd in, against her Inclination, and gaz'd on like a Malefactor ?

2*ly*. Stage Princes are used agreeably to their Station : The Honour of their Function shines out in their Appearance. Their very Misfortunes are Majestick, and their Ruin Glorious. They are never represented Insignificant, treated with Contempt, and Play'd the Fool with in *Comedy*. If they were thus used, I question not but that the *Poets* and *Players* would quickly hear on't. 3*ly*.

3*ly*. If Princes were ufed as Ill as Priefts upon the Stage, they would not fuffer fo much by it. Princes are well guarded againft Dramatick Out-rage. They have Power to Punifh and to oblige. The Magnificence of their Courts, the Pomp and Parade of their Figure, brighten their Authority, and preferve a Regard. Thefe Circumftances glitter upon the fenfe, and ftrike an awe upon the Spirits of the People. They refresh their Character, and make them underftood. They prevent the fpreading of Fiction into Life, and keep a *Play-Houfe-Abufe* from being Acted in the Streets. In fine; Wealth and Power tho much fhort of Princes, breaks the force of Infolence, and is a Sovereign Remedy againft Neglect. But the Clergy have no great fhare of thefe Advantages; I mean generally fpeaking, and with Us efpecially. Their Provifion is often flender, their Cenfures relate to another World, and they have nothing of Luftre to affect the Imagination. A Condition thus unfortified, thus unornamented, lies open to Ill ufage. The greater part of the Clergy are not fo well provided to difprove an unfair Reprefentation. They can't fo eafily confute a Calumny by their Equipage, nor make their Fortune put a Lye out of Countenance. To be taken notice of, Things muft fhine as well as be

folid;

folid ; a Coarſe out-ſide keeps the Richneſs within from being regarded. Spiritual Privilege, and inviſible Advantage ſignifie little with Ignorance, or Atheiſm. When a Man can ſcarce hold his Head above Water, there needs no great Weight to ſink him. Misfortune in ſuch an Age as this, is almoſt a Jeſt of it ſelf. A little Buffooning is ſufficient to make Indigence look ridiculous; for when a Man's Coat is threadbare, 'tis an eaſy matter to pick a hole in't.

4ly. His pretence of Matter of Fact is vid. St. *Auguſt*. De. Civ. Dei. Plin. pan Dio. Jul. Capitol. Hiſt. Auguſt. p. 27. Tacit. Annal. Vid. Serres Hiſt. Goſſon.

4ly. His pretence of Matter of Fact is not True. Princes *have complained of the Theater.* The great *Scipio* pull'd it down; *Trajan* & *Antoninus Philoſophus* diſcouraged *Plays*, and *Tiberius* Baniſhed the Stage. To come nearer Home, *Lewis* the Godly would not endure a *Play-Houſe,* and Queen *Elizabeth* often check't this ſort of Diverſion. Now theſe were moſt of them *Great Princes*, and which is more to the purpoſe, moſt of them good ones too.

Mr. *Congreve* ſeems now fallen into a fit of Levelling. Quality and Secular advantage, are grown *Bells* and *Baubles*. In his Logick, Honour and Eſtate, are Inconſiſtent with *Humility and other Chriſtian Virtues. Such Temporal Pride he pretends agrees very ill with the Perſon and Character of a truly Pious and Exemplary Divine.* Had this Gen-

P. 73.

Ibid.

Gentleman the Direction of Affairs, 'tis likely the World would be well mended, the Church Reformed into Apostolical Poverty, And all these *Antichristian* Things *of* Fortune and Convenience, taken from the *Exemplary Divines*, and given to the *Exemplary Poets*.

Mr. *Congreve* comes on again reinforced with Mr. *Hales*, who proves from Scripture that all " claim to superiority by Title of " *Christianity* is most certainly cut off. With submission to Mr. *Hales*, this is not universally true For the Church being a *Society*, must by consequence have Governours, and these by the same Necessity, must in that respect be superiour to the Governed. For this reason, the Apostle, speaking to private Christians, Enjoyns them in these words, *Obey them that have the Rule over you, and and submit your selves; for they watch for your Souls*, &c. This Text we see plainly contains a branch of Duty to *Ecclesiastical* Governours. Now those *who have the Rule over others*, are certainly so far their Superiors ; And those who are to *submit themselves*, are bound to acknowledge them as such. To go on with Mr. *Congreve*'s Citation. " Nature and Religion agree in this, " that neither of them has a hand in this " *Heraldry* of *secundum sub & supra* ; all this " comes from Composition and Agreement

" of

[margin: Amend. P. 74.]

[margin: Heb. 13. 17.]

Ibid. "of Men among themselves. Here Mr.
Hales is mistaken again; For Parents have
by Nature a Right of Superiority over their
Children. I grant Mr. *Hales*'s Principle
holds true in the Main; but nothing can be
more extravagant than Mr. *Congreve*'s Inference. Does this Gentleman mean that
there's no such thing as Superiority amongst
Christians? Is subordination destroyed by
Baptism? Does Christianity confound all
Degrees, and melt down all Distinction in
the *State*; This Doctrine is calculated for
Sleidan. the Meridian of *Munster*, for the *Boars* of
Comment. *Germany*, for *John* of *Leyden* and *Knipper-
dolling*: *Jack Straw* and *Wat Tyler*, *Cade* and
Ket would have been wonderfully obliged
at such a Discovery as this. But if Civil
Privileges are consistent with Christianity,
I hope the Clergy may plead their Right in
Common, and take the Advantage of the
Constitution like other People.

I had said, The *Addition of Clerk is at*
View, &c. *least equal to that of Gentleman; were it other-*
P. 136. *wise, the Profession would in many cases be a kind
of punishment.* I say so still. For if a Gentleman was made less, and degraded by going into *Orders*, would it not be a kind of
Punishment? Can any thing be plainer than
this? I can't imagine how Mr. *Congreve*
could misinterpret this Period. But since
he has done it, he would do well to call in
                                        his

his exclamation, and wonder at his own Ig- P. 75.
norance or Infincerity.

    I obferv'd, that *Monfieur Racine*, contrary
to the practice of foreign Countries, reprefented Priefts in his *Athalia*. I obferv'd
farther, That this *Play was a very Religious
Poem. And if it were not defign'd for the* View,&c.
Theater, I have nothing to object. My mean- P. 124.
ing is, if it were defign'd for the Theater,
I thought the Form and Argument too fo-
lemn for the Place. But that it was defign'd
for the *Theater*, is more than I know; and
I rather believe it was not. It being not
uncommon in *France* and elfewhere, to act
ferious and inoffenfive *Plays* in *Religious
Houfes.* Had Mr. *Congreve* underftood this,
or indeed the plain Englifh of the Words,
all his Cavilling and awkard Jefts had been
at an end. The *Short View*, &c. takes notice that *Shakefpear*, though to blame, was
a Genteeler Enemy than the *Relapfer* ; Why
fo? Becaufe he gives Sir *John*, Parfon of P. 125.
*Wrotham, fome Advantage in his Character,
he reprefents him Lewd, but not Little.* Here
Mr. *Congreve* is extreamly diverting. The
BUT (fays he) *is coming again. I had a* Amend.
glimpfe of him juft now. Beft of all; 'Tis more P. 74.
than he has of himfelf, fometimes. Lewd but
not Little, there's a Paradox for ye! Well,
I grant fome People are both. However,
there's room enough between thefe Qualities
for

for a Diſtinction. For I ſuppoſe a Man
may be Lewd in his Practice, without being Little in his Figure and Behaviour. Does
every Libertine wear a *Livery*, or is Lewdneſs a forfeiture of Condition ? In a ſenſe of
Philoſophy and Religion, there's nothing
meaner than Vice : But then the Advantage of Appearance is ſome Cover for the
Deformity, and gives it another Air to
Common View.

Mr. *Congreve* allows, That when *Men
neither Sneak, nor do any thing unbecoming
their Office in the World, they ought not to be*
P. 77.   *repreſented otherwiſe on the Stage.* Were the
Heathen Prieſts then ſo abſolutely unexceptionable ? Were there no Prevarications
amongſt them ? and did they never Live
out of their Character ? Mr. *Congreve* can't
think this : And yet as I obſerv'd, they
View, &c. were always well treated by the Heathen
P. 122.   Poets. But beſides, what occurs in this
Anſwer, I have given him my reaſons elſe-
View, &c. where, why the Clergy ought in no caſe to
come upon the Stage.

Mr. *Congreve* is ſo kind as to inform me,
that *I talk in the Pedantical Cant of Fable,
Intreague, Diſcovery, of Unities of Time*, &c.
P. 82.   He means the *Pedantical Cant* of *Ariſtotle*
and *Horace*, of *Boſſu* and *Corneille*, of *Rapin*,
and Mr. *Dryden* ; that is of the beſt Criticks,
both Antient and Modern, upon the Subject.

ject. This is somewhat strange ! But I perceive the Man is wildred in his Spleen: He
lost himself in a mist of his own making,
And when people can't see, they are apt to
fall foul upon their Friends.

He finds fault with some more expressi- P 84
ons of mine, how reasonably, I shall consider by and by.

Mr. *Congreve* having spent some Pages in
Trifling and Scurrility, advances to my *4th.*
Chapter. This *Chapter* charges the *Stage*
with Immorality for rewarding their loose
Characters, and giving their Libertines
such advantage in Figure, Sense and Suc-
cess. Mr. *Congreve* knew the *Old Batchelour* View,&c.
and *Double Dealer* concern'd under this Head, P. 142.
but takes no notice of it. 'Tis true, he makes
an attempt to disengage *Valentine* in *Love* Amend.
for Love. He would gladly Blanch this P. 38.
foul Character ; But alas, 'tis to no purpose
to wash and rub : The Spots are not Dirt
but Complexion. He says *Valentine had honesty enough to close with a bad Bargain, rather then not pay his Debts.* Thus Mr. *Congreve.* But if we will take *Valentine's* word
for't, we shall find the matter otherwise.
'Twas his Necessity, his disrelish of Confinement, his Passion for *Angelica,*which put
him upon this Complyance. Let him speak
for himself.

G   *Val.*

Val. *This Condition was once proposed before*
Lo.for Lo.
P. 8. 16. *and I refused it, but the present impatience of*
my Creditors for their Money, and my own im-
patience of Confinement, and absence from An-
gelica, force me to consent.

So much for his Honesty. And that he
is Debauch'd, Profane and Smutty, Unnatu-
View, &c.
P. 142. ral to his Son, and Undutiful to his Father,
I still affirm and appeal for Evidence to the
Pages of the Citation.

P. 41, 35.
Amend.
P. 90, 92. Mr. *Congreve* endeavours to justifie *Bell-*
mour and *Sharper,* in the *Old Batchelour,* a-
gainst my exceptions. But here according
to his usual fair dealing he misreports the
P. 92. Case. He tells the *Reader* I produc'd these
Passages to prove him guilty of *encouraging*
Immorality. But this is quite mistaking the
Matter. These Passages among others were
produced to show how roughly the *Women*
See View,
&c.P.165,
170, 171,
172. were treated by the *Stage* : That their fine
Characters were unceremonious, and fail'd
in the Decencies, of a *Cavalier.*

He is glad *I can prevail with my self to*
Amend.
P. 91. *write the Hellish Syllable* [POX] *at length;*
I could not do so in Page 82 of my Book.
Right. And I had some reason for my
Scruple. For I conceive, there is some dif-
ference between the naming a Blasphe-
mous Curse, and the Foul Disease. The
Word was used the former way when I de-
clin'd to transcribe it.

I

I have assaulted the Town, it seems, *in the seat of their principal and most reasonable Plea-* P. 105. *sure.* I am sorry to hear the encouraging of Vice, the Liberties of Smut, and Profaneness, the Exposing of Holy Things and Persons, are such lively satisfactions. The Palate must be strangely vitiated to relish such Entertainment as this. I would gladly believe the *Stage* has not yet subdued the Understandings of the *Audience,* nor debauched their Reason to this degree. I hope the *Town* is misreported in some measure, and that as to the choise and value of Pleasure, the *Psalmist's* Authority may be better than Mr. *Congreves, Blessed is the man that stands not in the way of Sinners, nor sits in the Seat* Psal. 1. 1, 2. *of the Scornful. But his delight is in the Law of the Lord.*

Mr. *Congreve* pretends the *Invectives of the Fathers were levell'd at the Cruelty of the* Gladiators, *and the Obscenity of the* Pantomimes. *If some of them,* continues he, *have confounded the* Drama *with such Spectacles, it was an oversight of Zeal very alowable in those Days; and in the Infancy of Christianity, when the Religion of the* Heathens *was Intermingled* P. 105. *with their* Poetry *and Theatral Representations.* The Fathers Censure of the *Stage,* of which I gave many Instances, *was an oversight of Zeal!* Their Heat ran away with their Judgment, and to make them safe, we must read
them

them with Mr- *Congreve*'s Comment. And yet this *oversight* of *Zeal* is forgotten, and their Conduct justified by our Author immediately after. For as the case then stood, he says *the best of the Heathen Plays might* *very well be forbidden.* But these Restraints, it seems were put upon *the Infancy of Christianity.* Under favour, *Christianity* was no gradual *Religion.* 'Twas like *Adam* at its full growth at first. If weakness, if obstinacy, and perverseness, are signs of *Infancy*, we are much more in the state of the *Cradle* now. As for the Concern of the *Heathen Religion*, that was not the only Objection the *Fathers* had to the *Stage.* They likewise Declaim'd against the Lewdness and Immorality of those Diversions. This I have shewn sufficiently in the Testimonies Cited from them : And likewise prov'd the Censure of the *Fathers* applicable to the *English* *Theater.*

Ibid.

View,&c.
P. 276.
deinc.

Mr. *Congreve* would gladly throw his own Talent of unfair Citing and Misapplying upon me. But has not been able to prove it in one Instance, excepting that mistake of *Wasting* for *Wafting* mentioned before.

Amend.
p.105.

P.106,107

His Story out of *Polybius* will do him no kindness ; for, as I have observed already, there is no Arguing from *Heathenism* to *Christianity.* Ignorance when not affected, goes a great way in an excuse. *Polybius* was a
wise

wise Man, but he was a Pagan, and lived
too early to know any thing of our Religion. In short, either the *Theatral Performances* of the *Cynethians* were innocent, or
they were not. If they were not, to what
purpose are they mention'd : If they were,
our Stage is no *parallel* to them. There being very few modern *Plays* in which there is
not something exceptionable: Either Cursing or Swearing, vain invocation of the
Name of God, Ribaldry, or Profaneness;
or else some foolish and destructive Passion
made Creditable and Charming. And as
for the Bulk of his Author *Polybius*, I suppose *Scipio Nasica*, *Scævola*, and St. *Augustin*,
were all of them as great Men as He. I shall
give him counter-Evidence from them. This
Father informs us, that *Scævola* who was St Aug. de
Pontifex Maximus, and one of the Senate, Civ. Dei.
dissuaded that *Noble Assembly from going on* lib. 1. cap.
with the Building of a Theater. He told them 31.
in a set Speech, *That this Diversion would
bring in Foreign Vice; and the Debaucheries
of* Greece *among them. That the old* Roman
*Virtue would be lost, and the Spirits of the Peo-
ple emasculated.* This Harangue govern'd
the *Senate,* and stopt the Progress of the *Stage*
for that time. This Testimony St. *Augustin*
mentions with Approbation. And in the
next Chapter but one, He calls these *Theatral* c:p 33.
Performances, animorum labem & pestem,

pra-

probitatis & honestatis eversionem, i. e. *The
Blemishes of Humane Nature, the Plague of
Reason, and the Ruine of Virtue* : And adds,
That *Scipio foreseeing these mortal consequences,
hindred the building of* Play-Houses. *He did not
think the Government could subsist upon the
strength of Brick and Stone. But that Discipline
and good Manners were to be taken care of no less
than the Fortification of the City*.

To the Authority of this Father I shall
Subjoyn that of *Horace*, vvho in his Book
de Arte Poetica, Mentioning the *Roman*
Theater before his ovvn Time, has these
vvords.

*Quo sane populus numerabilis ut pote parvus.
Et frugi, castusq; verecundusq; coibat.*

'Tis very remarkable says *Monsieur Dacier*, that *Horace* should commend the old
Romans for not frequenting the *Theater*. He
gives four Reasons for the little Inclination they had for these Diversions. " They
" vvere not very Numerous ; They vvere
" Wise ; They vvere Religious ; And they
" vvere Modest.

The three last Reasons are strongly to
our point, and the stronger for coming from
a *Poet*. This vvas so plain, and so Con-
siderable an acknovvledgment, that Mr. *Dacier* makes the follovving *Marginal* Note
upon it. *The Theater Condemned as inconsistent
with Prudence and Religion*.

*Dacier
Remarq
sur L' Art
Poetique
Vol. 10.
P. 238.*

*Ibid. Vol.
10. P. 37.*

As

As for innocent Diversions, I have nothing to say against them. But I think People should take care not to relieve their Spirits at the expence of their Virtue, not to Cure *Melancholy* with Madness, and shake off their Spleen, and their Reason together. Mr. *Gosson* a Stage Poet in Queen *Elizabeth*'s time says much the same thing, only the expression is somewhat stronger. In his Address to the *Gentlewomen* of *London*, he has these words: *Being pensive at Home, if you go to the Theaters to drive away Fancies, it is as good Physick, as for the Ache of your Head, to knock out your Brains; or when you are Stung with a Wasp, to rub the Sore with a Nettle.* SeeGoss.'s School of Abuse.

The same Author is so Frank as to declare, That *Ease and Idleness bring Destruction* ; and that *Pleasure and Sport are the Devil's Baits: That honest Recreation quickens the Spirits, but Plays are venemous Arrows to the Mind. When Comedy comes upon the Stage,* Cupid *sets up a Springe for Woodcocks, which are entangled e're they discern the Line, and caught before they mistrust the Snare.* And a little before, *We call that a Slaughter House where brute Beasts are kill'd, and hold that a Pastime which is the very Butchery of Christian Souls.* Apol. of the School of Abuse, p. 88,89.

Mr. *Congreve* argues at last from the disadvantage of the *Globe*, and the *uncertainty of our Climate.* Now I'm afraid these Geographical Reasons are no better than the rest. p. 108.

I doubt this Expedient of a *Play-house* won't
make the *Latitude* one jot the better. 'Twill
ne're fix the floating of our Humours, nor
bring us to the steddiness of the *Continent*.
To speak softly : What is there more likely
to awaken our Passions than these Diversions, and to fill us with Freaks and Fancies,
and extravagant Amusement ? Now when
Passions runs high, Disappointment rises with
them, and good Humour grows more pre-
carious. For the more we are disappointed,
the more *dark*, and *Saturnine*, and *Melancholick* we shall certainly be. The Resigna-
tion of Christians, and the Pleasures of Reason, and the Satisfaction of living to some
purpose, are by much, the best Remedies
against Melancholy. But *are not we of all
People the most unfit to be alone?* The French
Proverb shall answer this : *Better be Alone,
than in ill Company.* Mr. *Congreve* goes on in
his Panegyrick upon his Country : *Are there
not more Self-Murtherers, and Melancholick
Lunaticks in* England, *heard of in one year,
than in a great part of* Europe *besides.* Tho'
I somewhat question the Truth, as well as
the Civility of this Reflection; but if 'tis
true, 'tis probable the *Play-House* may in
some measure account for the *Fact*. If there
are more Self-Murthers and Lunacies in *England* than elsewhere, 'tis probably, because
there are more bad Plays in *England than in*

P. 10 .

Ibid.

a great part of Europe *besides* : I believe I
may say, than in all *Europe* besides. When
Passions are rais'd, and Principles destroy'd,
some People can neither keep their Wits,
nor their Lives long together. They grow
impatient of this World, and Foolish enough
to rush blindly upon the Other. *Love* and
Pride are observ'd to stock *Bedlam.* Now
these two Passions are work'd up to the
highest Excess in *Plays.* A Spark is scarce
thought Civil to his Mistriss, unless he's
ready to run Mad for her. And as for Pride,
'tis no less strongly recommended under the
Notion of Glory, Greatness, and Revenge.
Indeed the *Play-house* is a sort of Nursery to
a Mad House : 'Tis not long since one of
them was sent thither; and I rather wonder
they are not oftner transplanted. I am sorry
for any Man's Misfortune; and 'tis only
Mr. *Congreve*'s Argument which draws the
Instance from me. He is now come to his
last Questions. *From whence are all our Sects,* p. 109.
Schisms, and innumerable Subdivisions in Re-
ligion ? Let them come from whence they
will, we had better have them than
some Peoples Remedies. 'Tis much safer
to be of different Opinions, than agree in
believing nothing. Atheism is an ill Cure
of Heresy and Schism : I admire Uniformity
in Doctrine extreamly; but still I must crave
leave to believe, That a mistaken Conscience

enee is more serviceable, than no Confcï-ence at all.

Ibid. Mr. *Congreve* concludes his Book with an unfair Quotation about Musick. He under-stands the Art of Misrepresenting, and leaves out a significant *word*, very handsomly for that purpose. But I shall pass it over; and come to his Criticisms upon some of my Expressions.

p. 84. The *Ladies fancy Slip-stocking high* , with Echard's Reasons of the Con. of the Clergy. which he quarrels, is an Allusion to a known Story, in a Book very well known. To deal freely, I made bold with it to prevent its falling into the Enemies hand. *A whole Kennel of Beaus after a Woman*, is no Lan-Ibid. guage of mine: 'Tis a Quotation from the *Relapse*; as Mr. *Congreve* might easily have See View, &c. p 225 Relapse, p. 64. View,&c. p. 27. seen. *Running Riot upon Smut*, is misquo-ted. My words are these: " The *Double* " *Dealer* runs Riot upon such an occasion " as this, and gives Lord *Touchwood* a mix-" ture of *Smut*, &c. *The upper End of the Go-vernment*, is a defensible Expression; And his exception to the *Litter of Epithets*, &c. I have answer'd already. His Objections at *Big-Allyances*, is somewhat unfairly tran-scrib'd, and the Page mismark'd. The Pas-View,&c. p. 130. sage is this : " *Jehoida* was thought an Ally-" ance big enough for the Royal Family. He Cavils at two other little words, which I think may pass : But I shall say nothing in in their behalf. To defend such trifles, would be almost as idle, as to object against them.

Now though I have examined Mr. *Congreve's* Writings but loosely upon this Head, yet in return to his Civilities, I shall present the Reader with some Proprieties of His in Phraseology and Sense. In his Amendments P. 11. we have, To *Savour of Utterance*, &c. And in the *Mourning Bride*, we have all the Deli- p. 3. 79. cacies of Language and Rhetorick, and the very Spring it self upon Paper. Here's *Respiring Lips, ample Roof, and ample Knowledge*, M. Bride, *the Noon of Night, fear'd*, for frighted, the p. 24, 64, *pageantry of Souls, Eyes rain Blood*, and what 61, 57, 14. not. To go on a little with the *Mourning* P. 8. *Bride*, with reference to Sense and Character.

King *Manuell* asks his Daughter *Almeria*, why she wears Mourning at his Triumph. She tells him, *She mourns for her deliverance from a Wreck.* This was a wise Answer, and a very natural way of expressing her Gratitude for coming safe on Shore.

Gonsalez relates *Manuall's* Victorious Entry after his Success against the Moors. The Cavalcade is wonderfully Splendid and Pompous: But the Story goes off somewhat unluckily.

The swarming Populace spread every Wall, p. 7.
And cling as if with Claws they did enforce
Their Hold through clifted Stones stretching and
staring.
Here

Here he Struts to purpose in *Sophocles*'s Buskins! *Cling* and *Claws* are extreamly magnificent in solemn Description, and strangely proper for Tragedy and Triumph. To give him his due, I think these two Lines are the best Image of a parcel of Cats running up a Wall, that I have met with. That which follows is worth the remembring.

Ibid.   *As they were all of Eyes, and every Limb,*
Would feed his Faculty of Admiration.

A Limb of an Eye, I confess, is a great Curiosity; And one would think if the *Poet* had any of these Limbs in his Head, he might have discover'd it. We must not forget *Osmin*'s Talent in Arithmetick, who let us understand that

p. 21.   *Heaven can continue to bestow,*
When scanty Numbers shall be spent in telling.

As Scanty as they are, I *fancy Telling* will be spent much sooner than *Numbers* : But Sense in a Tragedy is cold and unaffecting. To go on. *Zarah* makes *Osmin* a high Compliment upon his Air and Complexion : She tells him when she first saw him,

p. 23, 24.   *Pale and expiring, drenched in briny Waves,*

That

That he was
God-like even then.

Death and Palenefs are ftrong Refem-
blances of a Deity! But I perceive, to fome
People, a Seraphim, and a drown'd Rat, are
juft alike. King *Manuell* is giving Sentence
upon the Rebels: Let us fee how he fup-
ports his Character:

Bear to the Dungeon thofe Rebellious Slaves,   p. 41.
The ignoble Curs that Yelp to fill the Cry,
And fpend their Mouths in barking Tyranny.

And a little after, he calls the Noble *Ofmin,*
that foreign Dog. Here's Majeftick Paffion,
Royal Vengeance, and magnificent Railing
for ye! A Common Hunt could not have
done it better! This, as Mr. *Congreve* has   Amend.
it, is *Dog-Language* with a Witnefs; and   p. 28.
never made for a Monarch's Mouth.

    Zara has another Flight very remarkable,
and with that I fhall conclude. This Prin-
cefs, we muft know, was ftrangely fmitten
with *Ofmin,* and finding her Amour crofs'd,
was refolv'd, out of ftark Love and Kind-
nefs, to Poifon him: 'Tis true, fhe intended
to be fo juft, as to difpofe of her felf the fame
way. Now coming to the Prifon fhe fpies
a Body without a Head, and imagining it *Of-*
min's, grows diftracted upon't. And why
                     fo?

fo ? Was it becaufe fhe was prevented, and had not the fatisfaction of difpatching her Spark her felf? Or was it becaufe fhe had a mind to convince *Ofmin* of the ftrength of her Affection by murthering him? That's fomewhat odd. Was it then to fhew how willing fhe was to dye with him? She fays fo ; but prefently rejects this reafon as frivolous and unneceffary. For if you'll believe her, *Ofmin* was capable of knowing her Paffion, without fo barbarous an Expedient.

P. 63. *His Soul ftill fees, and knows each purpofe,*
    And fixt event of my perfifting Faith.

Well, Let the reafon of her Diforder be what it will, for we can't agree about it, fhe falls into a moft terrible Fit of Fuftian , upon the fight of the Body.

P. 62. *Ha ! proftrate ! bloody ! headlefs ! O, --- ftart Eyes,*
    Split heart, burft every Vein at this dire object ;
    At once diffolve and flow ; meet Blood with Blood,
    Dafh your encountring Streams with mutual Violence,
    Till Surges roll, and foaming Billows rife,
    And curle their Crimfon Heads to kifs the Clouds!

One would think by this Rant, that *Zara* had Bloud enough in her Veins to fill the *Bay* of *Bifcay*, or the Gulph of *Lions*. At
this

this fate a Man may let the *Thames* out of his little Finger! This is monstrous Impropriety of Thought! Never were Things and Words, joyn'd more unluckily. Call you this Poetry! The Figures and Flights of Poetry are Bold; but then the Fancy should be Natural, the Figures Just, and the Effects holds some proportion with the Cause. *Zara* rises in her Rumbling, if 'tis possible, rails bitterly on the King, in *Astronomy*; And, as far as I can discover, she goes somewhat upon the System of *Copernicus*.

Rain, rain, ye Stars spout from your burning P. 62 *Precipitated Fires, and pour in Sheets,* [*Orbs,* *The blazing Torrent on the Tyrant's Head.*

Well. Tho this Lady has not much Wit in her Anger, she has a great deal of Learning: I must own, this is a very Scholar-like piece of Distraction. If Mr. *Congreve* replies, the Occasion was extraordinary; and that the sight of *Osmin*'s Murther must mightily affect her. Granting all this, the old Saying will hold good against him: *Curæ leves loquntur, ingentes stupent:* Here *Almeria*'s Fit of Fainting, and a good Swoon at the end on't, would have look'd like Business, and P. 37. been very Natural upon the occasion. I could have been somewhat larger upon the *Mourning Bride*, but this may suffice at present.

I

I charged Mr. *Congreve* with two very Lewd and Scandalous Songs; but thefe he paffes over unmention'd. This is fomewhat unfortunate: One would have thought, if he had neither Modefty to make them, nor Reafon to defend them, he might, at leaft, have had a little Confcience to have given them up.

View,&c.
P. 24, 25.
L. for L.
Lov. Tri-
umph. p.
73.

A Reply

A
REPLY

TO THE

Short Vindication

OF THE

Relapse and the *Provok'd-Wife*.

THIS Author pretends I had little to charge him with upon the Subject of Immodesty, that *I come to no particulars*, but only mention *Miss Hoyden with others for an Immodest Character*. By his favour, I am particular in the matter objected, and since he calls for it, I shall direct the *Reader* to some more Decencies of this young Lady. To deny Matter of Fact in the beginning of a Vindication is a little unlucky!

Vindic. P. 7.

View, &c. P. 221.

Relapse p. 60, 62, 63.

This Gentleman is at *a loss what I mean by Immodesty, he knows of no smut talked by Miss Hoyden;* And makes the Fault mine to understand him in that sense. Here's a flight of In-

Ibid.

nocence

nocence for ye! One would think his Capacity was bound up to Virtue in an extraordinary manner ; And that the bare Notion of Ill could not get into his Head. By the way, I am sorry to find him thus Undistinguishing. This Ignorance in a *Stage-Poet* does not look well. Customary Swearing takes away the sense of doing it, and I am afraid it may be applicable to other matters. The *Vindicator* and his Brethren have an admirable way of defending themselves from Indecencies. If you detect them, they tell you 'tis your own Construction, *and you may take it for your pains.* As if the Knowledge of Good and Evil, was Criminal ; and to show one Fault, was to make another. It seems then the Deformity of Matters lies in the *Organ*, not in the Object, in the Idea not in the Thing. A Man had much better go into a Puddle than discover it. He that sees an Ulcer, or perceives an offensive Smell, is extreamly to blame in his Senses! The *Vindicator* imposes on the *Reader* by affirming himself *concern'd only in one Quotation more* in my Chapter of *Immodesty.* For

Ibid.

1. The general Reference may imply more. And besides, if it did not, I have given more Instances in *Loveless* and *Berinthia*, on the same Head, tho not in the same *Chapter*. There are likewise more lewd Passages in his two *Plays* heighten'd with Irreligion; but these shall be Postpon'd a little.

View, &c.
P. 219,
220.

Relapse, p.
47, 51, 73,
74.

I shall now examine his Defence of a quotation from the *Provok'd-Wife.* The Dialogue lies between Lady *Brute* and *Belinda. Belinda* says, *Why dont some Reformer or other beat the Poet for Smuttiness?*
L. *Brute,*

P. 41.

L. Brute, *Because he is not so sure of our Private Approbation; as of our Publick Thanks. Well; sure there is not upon Earth, so Impertinent a thing as Womens Modesty.*

Belind. *Yes, Mens Fantasque that obliges us to it. If we quit our Modesty, they say we lose our Charms.* (There's his Defence.) *And yet they know that very Modesty is Affectation, and rail at our Hypocrisy.* Here's admirable encouragement for Virtue! The Ladies make a Grievance of Modesty, and declare it the most impertinent thing in Nature. Ay, but what do the Men say? Why they say 'tis all Affectation and Hypocrisie. And are not these Charming Qualities upon the Discovery? A pretence seen through is wonderfully engaging! The *Vindicator* confesses as much. He says the Men rail at the Women for their Modesty. I can't see how they should do otherwise, if they believe it nothing but Grimace. Here's a handsome Complement upon the Women. They are brought in guilty by both *Sexes*, They can't be Sincere it seems without appearing Vitious, nor deal clearly without Impudence, nor be Honest without playing the Whore! But over and above the *Poets* Courtship; these are Powerful Motives to Modesty! What Woman would not be in Love with it upon this Description? The Credit of Affectation is strangely transporting, who would not take pains to be counted a Hypocrite? There's nothing of Complexion in Modesty: 'Tis only a little Paint laid on with a Trowel. It neither sits easie, nor looks natural: 'Tis foolish to them-

selves,

felves, and formal to other People : And now
what Woman would not ſtrive hard for ſuch
an Accompliſhment as this ? But on the other
ſide, this is a comfortable Scheme for the
Town Sparks. To ſpeak in our Author's Mi-
litary way. What Libertine would not preſs
the Siege, and be at the trouble of a little
Storming, when he has Intelligence of a Party *within* ; when he believes the *Bloody-Colours*
falſe, and that there's Friendſhip in the very
Defiance ? Now had I not upon this Occa-
ſion ſome reaſon to obſerve that Modeſty was
out of Faſhion with our *Stage*, and the *Bank*
much ſunk ſince the time of *Euripides*, I ſay
ſince the time of *Euripides* ; For his Ladies
always converſe with all the Decency and Re-
ſervedneſs imaginable. They declare againſt
intemperate Talk, and love Virtue both in
the Thing and in the Appearance.

I had ranged the *Profaneneſs* of the *Stage* under two Heads.

1. *Their Curſing and Swearing*.
2. *Their Abuſe of Religion and Holy Scriptures*.

Upon the Head of *Swearing*, I obſerv'd the
Relapſe and the *Provok'd-Wife*, were particularly *Rampant* and *Scandalous*. This, the *Vindicator* ſays, was done with a great deal of
Honeſty and *Charity*. So 'twas. To report
fairly, and tell People of their Faults, is very conſiſtent with both thoſe Qualities. He
goes on, and jeſts a little about *Bullys* and
Hackney-Coach-men, and by the Gayety of his
Humour, you would think him extreamly
Innocent. But after all this unconcernedneſs,
if

Vind.P.11

if his Crime should not be little, I am afraid
his Conscience will appear so. However he
complains he is mightily overcharg'd; and
that *all the stretch of the Prophaneness lies in*
Ld. Foppington's *Gad, and* Miss Hoyden's
I-Cod. Now *Hoyden's* Expression I take to be Vind.p.11
rank *Swearing*, neither does he deny it. And
as for Ld. *Foppington*, he adds *By*, to *Gad*;
which in his particular way of Pronouncing
o, like *a*, is broad and downright. This Gentleman would excuse himself by the Liberties of Conversation, and gives several Instances of disguised Oaths. What means he by
insisting so much upon Precedent ? Does Custom justifie a Fault? Is Sin Improv'd into
Privilege ? and can a Man *Swear* by *Common-
Law* ? Besides all the Instances mention'd ex-   View,&c.
cepting *Par Die*, are less Criminal than his   P. 96. An.
own. And were it otherwise, no sort of Pro-   Cong. vid.
faneness is fit for Representation; as I have   3d. Post.
prov'd sufficiently already. This Author com-   P. 10.
plains, *my Accusations against him almost always run in general Terms*, &c. Well. If a
List of Particulars will oblige him, he shall
have it. I did not take this Method for want
of Evidence, I can assure him. The petty Oaths
and Curses (as I suppose the *Poets* think them)
together with the vain Invocation of the
Name of God, I shall omit; To transcribe
or point to them, would be tedious. But as
for those of a blacker Complexion, tho they
must not be produced, the *Reader* may see
them if he pleases : And then he may judge
if I have done the *Vindicator* any wrong by
pronouncing them *Rampant* and *Scandalous*.

In

In the *Relapse* this Horrible Rhetorick is spoken by Ld. *Foppington*, *Young Fashion*, *Seringe*, *Coupler*, and *Miss Hoyden*.   To these we must add *Justice Tunbelly*, who to make himself the better Magistrate, Swears like a *Bully* with open Mouth.   The *Provok'd-Wife* is little better.   Sir *John* and the *Colonel* Swear with a great deal of Relish and Noise; and *Constant* is not over stanch.   Some of these Pages have double Charges, and so have some in the *Relapse*.   Cursing and *Fiends* Language, is likewise very frequent in the *Provok'd-Wife*. Now, tho Oaths are not, Curses may be *Blasphemy*, *Fashion's* is so in a horrible manner.   This fine Gentleman does not stick to Curse the Author of his Being, for making him younger than his Brother.   But this is not all the *Blasphemy* the *Relapser* has to account for. And now at the close of the Article I must own my self surpriz'd at the Courage of the *Vindicator*.   That a Man thus Ill prepar'd, should cast the Cause upon so bold an Issue, press for a second Hearing, and call for a Charge in Particulars !

The *second* Branch of the *Stage's* Profaneness, is the Abuse of *Religion* and *Holy Scripture*.   How does the *Vindicator* excuse himself here ? He says, *Before he fell upon me for an Abuser of* Holy Scripture, *he should first clearly have prov'd, That no Story, Phrase or Expression whatsoever in the* Scripture, *should be either repeated, or so much as alluded to upon the Stage*. In return to this, I must say, I have hinted this pretty strongly already, and proved it by plain Implication.   To argue the

Relapse P.
7,9,11,13,
28,32,33,
43,44,55,
61,62,65,
66,74,75,
77,78,81,
87, 101,
102, 103,
105.
P10. Wife.
P. 20,27,
36,37, 39,
76.

Relapse p.
44.

P. 13.
View, &c.
Ch. 2.

point

point more at length, I did not then think ne-
ceſſary. For what can be more evidently Impious than to throw the moſt Solemn and the
moſt Trifling things into the ſame Compo-
ſition; to make *Religion* part of our Sport,
and the *Bible* furniſh out the Stage ? I
thought no Perſon profeſſing Chriſtianity,
could have wanted Information in this Caſe.
But ſince I find the *Poets* diſpoſed to Cavil,
I have ſatisfied this Objection more at large in
my *Reply* to Mr. *Congreve*. The *Vindicator*'s
next attempt is very remarkable.

See 4th.
Poſtul.

The Scripture, ſays he, *is made up of Hiſtory,
Prophecy, and Precept ; which are things in their
own Nature capable of no other Burleſque than
what calls in queſtion either their Reality, or their
Senſe.* To this I Anſwer,

P. 14.

1ſt. That the *Vindicator* is out in his Notion of *Burleſque*. To *Burleſque* a Book, is to
turn it into *Ridicule*. Now this may be done
without queſtioning the Hiſtory, or miſtak-
ing the *Text*. To apply the Caſe : To doubt
the Meaning of ſome part of the *Bible* may
be done without a Fault. I confeſs, to queſtion any *Facts* in *Scripture* would be to re-
nounce *Chriſtianity*. But then to make Diverſion with them is ſtill worſe ; And adds
Contempt, to Infidelity. Indeed, to take theſe
Freedoms with Religion is a ſign of a ſlender
Belief. We don't ſee *Comedy* Garniſhed with
Parliament-Houſe-Speeches. No. Where people are ſure to be *puniſhed*, they are careful not
to *provoke*.

2ly. To believe the *Scripture* God's Word,
and to play with it, heightens the Preſumpti-

H 4   on.

on. 'Tis a horrid Reflection on the Divine
Wisdom; It supposes the Concerns of the
other World over flourish'd, that a Pompous
out-side is given to Things Insignificant, and
that the weight of the Cause holds no proportion with the Solemnity of the Court. Now
that this Gentleman has several times brought
the *Bible* to jeft for him, is clear beyond
all Contradiction.

3*ly.* The *Vindicator* is caft upon his own
ftate of the Cafe. For his *Play* not only queftions the Truth of the *Scripture,* but denies
it; and gives an Inftance to prove the Af-
fertion; and to give the more Credit to't, it
comes from the beft Character in the *Poem.*
'Tis done in a Soliloquy too, where according to our Author, *the perfon who speaks is always suppofed to deliver his real thoughts to the Au-*
Vind.p.76 *dience. Amanda* is the perfon; Lets hear her.

What *slippery Stuff are Men Composed of?*
Relapse P. *Sure the Account of their Creation's false,*
97. *And 'twas the Womans Rib that they were form'd*
                                                            [*of.*

This Lady it seems fpoke this for the good
of the Publick; Her bufinefs, like *Worthy's,*
was to Inftruct the Audience. Yes, the defign of a *Soliloquy,* is to prevent mifconftru-
ction, to direct the Underftanding, and fecure
the Intereft of Virtue. 'Tis poffible the *Account of Man's Creation might have been thought
true,* and the meaning of the *Relapse* mifunder-
ftood, if *Amanda* had not been drawn out
fingle for this Service. Well. But *the Gentle-*
P. 21. *men who writ this Speech is gone to* Mufcovy.
I hope not to tell them the *Hiftory* of the Cre-
                                                            ation

ation is falſe ; well let him go, I think this *Town* may ſpare him.   But tho the *Man* is gone to *Muſcovy*, the *Play* is here, and ſo is the Author too, who took the pious *Muſe* into his Protection and made her Free of his *Poem.* Suppoſe this new *Lawreat* ſhould write a Treaſonable Copy of Verſes upon the *Czar*, and ſheer off from *Moſco* when he had done. Suppoſe a Brother *Poet* of the Place ſhould borrow them for his proper uſe, and Act and Publiſh them for his own. Would it be a ſufficient excuſe for the Latter to alledge that they were only borrowed, that his Friend was gone into a remote Country ; but *That to his Knowledge he had too much Veneration for the Government to queſtion its Authority, or ſink its Credit ?* I am afraid ſuch a Speech as this, would do but little Service at *Moſco.* It may not be amiſs for the *Vindicator* to conſider the Application, and the next time he has any *Exerciſe* made for him, to look a little better into the Contents.

We are now drawing towards Particulars. The Hiſtory of *Adam*'s Fall is wretchedly made uſe of in the *Provok'd-Wife*.   *How the* Scripture *is affronted by this*, the Vindicator *can't tell* ; *here's nothing that reflects upon the Truth of the Story*.   No.   Is the Ridiculous *Raſor* no diſadvantage to the Story ? Does it not ſuffer by being mix'd up with Smut and Banter, and applied to a ſcandalous purpoſe. If theſe Liberties don't reflect upon the *Truth* of the *Story*, I am ſure they reflect upon the Significancy on't, and by conſequence upon the Honour of the Author.   But by the *Vindicator's*

P. 77.
View, &c.
P. 77.
P. 14, 15

dicator's Favour, I doubt it does Reflect upon the *Truth of the Story*. For who that look'd on this Account as deliver'd by the *Holy Ghost* would treat it thus disrespectfully? Who that believed himself akin to *Adam* would use his Memory thus Coursely, Ridicule *his Folly* upon the *Stage*, and make a jest of his Misfortunes? The *Vindicator* concludes the Page with a Memorable Sentence, and gives us to understand, *That he shall always make a very great Distinction between his Respects to God and the Devil*. *His Respects to God*, is somewhat Familiar. But he mends the Matter. He makes a very great Distinction between God and the Devil! Then it seems he has some Regard for both of them, some Respects for the Devil. Truly one would almost think so, by his way of Writing, and if we may argue from the Interest he promotes, I am afraid the Bulk of the *Distinction* will lie the wrong way.

The *Vindicator* takes it Ill of me for Censuring the Liberties given to Ld. *Foppington*. And *here* (he says) *I'm as angry with him for being for Religion, as before for being against it*. Not altogether. However here's a frank Confession, that he was against *Religion* before. Now by his managing, one would guess he had not changed his side. For whatever his Meaning might be, his Method is somewhat untoward. For does not Ld. *Foppington* Droll upon the *Prayers*, upon *Sundays*, and *Sermons*? Does he not do it in Earnest? The *Vindicator* grants all this. Is he check't then by the Ladies, or expos'd upon the Account? Very slen-

Vind.P.15

Ibid.

P. 16.

slenderly, if at all. *Berinthia* rather prompts him, and *Amanda* only asks him if there was good *Preaching* at St. James's; *And that she* Relapse. P.
was the worst Company in the world at Church, 32, 33.
being apt to mind the Prayers and Sermon. This is a poor Rebuke for such Rampant Profaneness. And as the World goes, may eas- View, &c.
ly be interpreted to Singularity, and Female P. 78.
Superstition. Ay, *But* Foppington's *manner of speaking ; together with the Character he repre-sents plainly instructs the Audience, that what he* P. 16, 17.
says of his Church Behaviour is design'd for their Contempt and not for their Imitation. 'Tis de-signed for their Diversion, if he pleases, which I'm mistaken if the Subject will allow of. Let Ld. *Foppington* speak.

Ld. *Fop. Madam, Sunday is a vile day, I must confess ; I intend to move for leave to bring in a Bill that the Players may work upon it. —— A Man must have little to do there, that can give an account of the Sermon. —— But if I can't give an account of the Ladies, I deserve to be excommunicated. —There's my Lady Tattle,* &c. *are the prettiest* Relapse P.
Company in the World. —— One is strangely apt at 32, 33.
Church to mind what one should not do, meaning the *Prayers* and the *Sermon.*

Now who can miscarry under such Instru-ction as This? A Man must be of a very low Form in his Understanding, not to see the Drift of the *Author*. This is Seraphick Satyr, all Light and Heat. Virtue must needs be re-fresh'd, and Conscience alarm'd strongly, by such Admonitions! Instead of giving a fright-ful Idea of Profaneness, the Matter is all turn'd into a Jest; and the Audience desired to laugh

at

at thofe Practices, which will Damn them.
Thefe are admirable Sentences to Rally Religion with, to furnifh a young Libertine, and
keep Atheifm in Countenance ! So much for
the *Manner of Speaking*. And as for Lord *Foppington*'s Character, that won't excufe him.
As the Poet has manag'd the bufinefs, this
Lord is not fo contemptible. For fome of
the beft Raillery in the Play falls to his Share,
as I have fhewn already. And were it other-
wife, no pretence of Character can juftifie fuch
profane Sallies. But thefe Poets, if they can
get a Fool, a Bully, or a Libertine, to fly out
into Smut, or Irreligion, they are fafe enough.
Thus they can Pleafe and Fence, at the
fame time; and the *Character*, as they fancy,
is a Cover for the Trick. But there is much
more of Art than Fair-dealing, in this Expedient. I wifh they would confider, 'tis the
Poet that fpeaks in the *Perfons* of the Stage;
And that he who makes a Man Mad, muft anfwer for his Diftraction.

The *Vindicator can find no reafon for my Quarrel to Young Fafhion, unlefs 'twas becaufe I took
him for his Friend.* Then I was much to blame.
But the worft is, this Gentleman contradicts
himfelf in the next Sentence; and fays, *I accus'd his younger Brother, for kicking his Confcience
down Stairs.* Well. That's fomething; but not
all the Quarrel. I complain'd of him likewife
for a finifh'd Debauchee; and exhibited a long
Bill againft him. This the *Vindicator* is pleas'd
to flide over: And inftead of defending his
Libertine, finds fault with my calling him his
Favourite. And why fo? Has he not provided
him

Margin notes:
View, &c. P. 223.
View p. 96
Anfw. to *Congreve.*
P. 17.
View, &c. p. 210, 211
P. 18.

him a *Plot*, a *Fortune*, and a creditable Figure?
And are not all these signs of good Will and
Inclination? Well; but *his Wife is likely to* Ibid.
make his Heart ake. Indeed so says the *Vindi-*
cator. But *Young Fashion* tells another Story.
He is in no Fright about the matter. Upon
observing some Signs of Extravagance in *Hoy-*
den, he says to himself, (and then you may
be sure *he delivers his real Thoughts to the Audi-*
ence) *'Tis no matter. She brings an Estate will* Relapse,
afford me a separate Maintenance. We see here's P. 64.
no danger of Mortification. This Soliloquy
is extreamly Moral! It teaches the Art of
Marrying the Estate without the Woman, and
makes a Noble Settlement upon Lewdness.

The *Vindicator* complains because *I wont take* p. 18, 19.
his word in the business of Pimping. Under favour, he does me wrong; I never questioned
his Experience in these matters. Since he puts
me upon't, I am willing to believe him a good
Authority in the Case: And that he is well
qualified to pronounce upon the Growth and
Improvement of this Mystery. What if the
Profession soars somewhat higher than formerly, I
hope 'tis not grown creditable? If 'tis infamous in
a Peasant, 'tis more so in a Person of Figure?
Why then is it not Lash'd and Stigmatiz'd?
Why han't we some of *Plautus*'s and *Terence*'s
Discipline upon't? Why is the Poet's *Fine*
Gentleman put upon this Drudgery? To use See Pref.
the Profession thus gently, and pay it so fair a Relapse.
Respect, is the way to make it soar still *higher*,
and bring it more into Fashion. But the *Vin-*
dicator's Civilities to *Pimping* were not the only
Thing which I objected: I observ'd that *Wor-*
thy

thy and *Berinthia* made it an Act of *Christian*
Charity, and rallied profanely upon the Office.
But 'tis not this Gentleman's Method, to speak
to the Difficulty.

He tells me 'tis a dull Thing, to expect any
thing not dull from a *Nurse*.   And why so?
As slender People are entertaining sometimes.
Why mayn't the Woman be a little Witty if
she was Born so, especially when she is to divert the Company ? All Nurses are not Fools,
any more than all Poets are Wits.   Besides, I
did not expect any great matters from her in
this kind.   But though she has not Wit, she
ought to have Humour ? So that when she is
out of Character in her Profaneness, and speaks
contrary to Custom and Probability, when
the Race and Spirit of her Discourse, lies only
in the Abuse of Two or Three solemn Expressions of *Scripture*, I say when this happens,
'tis pretty plain the Poet's Design, is to treat
the Audience at the Expence of Religion.

The *Vindicator* sets down some more of
Nurses fine Speech which I had omitted. She
calls *Bull* Priest of *Baal*, and tells him, her *Conscience flies in her Face for taking his Advice ; and
that his Absolution is not worth an old Cassock.* Now
all these fine Sentences are only for Diversion.
'Tis nothing but *Cracking a Jest upon a Chaplain* ;
And he should *be very sorry to see the Day when
such a Liberty where it has no Allusion to Religion)
should be brought within the Verge of Profaneness.*
And how does he prove a Jest on a Chaplain
such a warrantable piece of Raillery ? Has not
a Chaplain the same Commission and Business
with another Clergyman ? And if so, why
should

Marginal notes:
View,&c.
p. 79,219.

p. 19.

Relapse,
p. 96.

P. 20.

Ibid.

should his Treatment be more Course? If there's no Distinction in the Office, why should there be any in the Usage? But it may be the *Vindicator* may think his Authority sunk upon the Score of Obligation: And that *Eating* and *Drinking*, are better than *Prayers* and *Sacraments*. But this passage of *Nurses has no Allusion to Religion*. That's strange! Is Sporting in Scripture-phrase, so foreign to that Subject? Has the Drolling on the Priests Blessing, upon the Power of the *Keys*, and the Institution of our Saviour, no Allusion to Religion? If this Gentleman had the Stating of Profaneness, 'twould shrink into a narrow Compass. It would be no easy matter to talk amiss; and the *Laity* would have as little Sin left them, as the *Clergy* would have fair Quarter. Ibid.

Worthy's Address to the fine Procuress *Berinthia*, must now be enquir'd into. Upon her promise of a Lewd Assistance, his Gratitude is wonderfully rais'd, and Devout. *Thou Angel of Light, let me fall down and adore thee.* He says, *if I had quoted her Answer, I had given a better Character of him; and he thinks, of my self.* Truly, I would gladly oblige both of us, but I'm afraid 'twon't do this time: However, let's hear *Berinthia*'s Answer. *Ber. Thou Minister of Darkness get up again; for I hate to see the Devil at his Devotions.* This is to make amends for t'other. I can't perceive how. One Man injures his Neighbour, and another blames him for't; does this cancel the guilt, & make the Fact nothing. One Man speaks Blasphemy, & another reproves him; does this justifie the Boldness, or make the Words unspoken? But by this

Vind. p 22
View, &c.
P. 80.

p. 23.

Relapse,
p 91.

An-

Vind. p. 23 *Answer the Audience are put in mind, she is not supposed to deserve that Compliment.* I can't see that neither. *Berinthia's* Answer looks rather like a design of carrying on the Profaneness, and continuing the Religious Banter. Her Character is loose throughout the *Play,* and she never says ought that's good, unless to abuse it. The Poet might easily see, that Instruction in her Mouth was most likely to be misunderstood and miscarry. There's no occasion for much quoting, the next Lines will shew us how significant her Advice must needs be.

Well, (*says* Worthy) *my incomparable Berinthia, how shall I requite you?*

Relapse.   Ber. *O ne'er trouble your self about that : Virtue* (alias Pimping) *is its own Reward. There's*
Ibid.   *a Pleasure in doing good, which sufficiently pays it self.* Here's a Lecture of Philosophy well apply'd ! This is an Admirable Lady to correct ill Sentences, and give Aim to the Audience ! And yet the jest on't is, the Man's not pleas'd because I did not commend him for his Care. Truly he must excuse me, I am not so full of *Panegyrick* as this comes to.

I cited L. *Brute* for saying *the Part of a downright Wife is to Cuckold her Husband.* The addition of *setting it down as a Precept,* is all his own, and so consequently is the *Foul Play* too, as will appear by the *Ladies* words.

Pro.-Wife   *Belinda ---- I could almost resolve to play the*
P. 3.   *downright Wife, and Cuckold him.* Is not to
View, &c. play the Knave, and to play the part of a
P. 83.   Knave the same thing ? This, tho it does not imply Duty and Precept, it supposes general

heral Practice, Truth in Notion, and propriety of Character: And as a Man cannot be
said to be a Knave, without playing Knavish
Tricks; so by the *Poets* Reasoning, a Woman
can't be said *to play the downright Wife*, unless
she Injures her Husband. This is a great Compliment to the Ladies! And whether the
Vindicator has reason *to ask their Pardons for*   Vind. p. 23
Lying, in jest or in earnest, the *Reader* must
judge.

He owns Lady *Brute* in her next Reply,
says, *that which at first View seems much more*   P. 24.
lyable to exception. This Confessiion is more
than ordinary; Let the Lady speak.

L. Brute, *Why, after all there's more to be said
for't* (for Adultery) *than you'd imagine Child.
I know according to the strict Statute Law of Religion, I should do wrong; but if there were a
Court of Chancery in Heaven, I should be sure to
cast him.*

Belind. *If there were a House of Lords you
might.*

L. Brute, *In either I should Infallibly carry my
Cause. Why he is the first Aggressor.* (It had been
worse if he had been the second.) *Not I.*

Belind. *Ay, but you know, we must return good*   P to. Wife.
for evil.   P. 4.

L. Brute, *That may be a mistake in the Tran-*   Vicw, &c.
slation.   P. 83.

Thus the Justice of God, the Court of Hea-
ven, and the Precepts of our *Saviour* are Ri-   S. Mat. 5.
diculed! And what can make satisfaction for
these horrible outrages? Not all the Blood
in a Man's Veins. The Mercy that Pardons
such Boldness, had need be infinite! But tho

Vin-

(114)

Vindicator has taken care *that her Raillery should*
not be mistaken for her serious Opinion. She **Ibid.**
tells *Belinda, I shall play the fool, and jest on,* **Pro.Wife.**
till I make you begin to think, I am in earnest. **p. 4.**
This is an admirable defence! The Woman
Blasphemes in jest, and diverts the Company
with the *Bible*, and therefore all's well; and **Ibid.**
the *Poet must be commended for his Caution!* I
perceive God and Religion are very Significant Things with some People!

Relapse P. To disengage *Young Fashion* from his very
19. Profane Application of *Providence.* He says,
View,&c. *every body knows the word* Providence *in common*
P. 84. *Discourse goes for Fortune.* A Man that's sink-
ing will catch at a Weed. I am sorry I
must spend my time about *words*, especially in so plain a Signification. But since the
business must be undertaken, I shall endea-
Cic. De. vour at a brief satisfaction. We may observe
Nat. Deor. then that *Tully* in his Philosophical Tracts di-
Lib. 1. P. stinguishes *Providence* from the *Epicurean* Sy-
4670,4671 stem of Chance and Fortune. *Providence* and
Lib. 2. P. *Divine Administration*, are with him the same
4732, Thing. The Emperour *Marcus Antonius Phi-*
4764. Ed. *losophus* has this Religious Expostulation. τί
Du. Pays. μοι τῶν ἐν κόσμῳ κενῶ θεῶν, κ᾽ πρενοίας κενῶ *Who*
would live in a World uninhabited by the Gods,
and Providence? Now for a little English Authority' Sir *Roger L' Estrange* in his *Æsop's*
Fables, uses the Word *Providence* frequently **P. 68, 78.**
for the Government of the World by the Dei- **& alib.**
ty; but no otherwise that I Remember. And
more particularly in the 187, and 211. Pages,
he makes the Notion of *Fortune* and *Providence*
distinct, and opposes the one to the other.

This

This Gentleman is well known to be a Master of Stile, and therefore I chuse to instance
in him. Mr. *Dryden* another good Judge in
Language, uses, *Providence* in the same Sense
tho not upon so good an Occasion. To Conclude. The *Relapser* himself shall come in
Evidence, and Attack the *Vindicator* for once.
Enter *Bull.*

Don Seba.
P. 51.

Mock Aft.
P. 36.

Relapse P.
97.

   Bull, What Providence orders, I submit to.
   Nurse, And so do I, with all Humility.
   Coupler, Why that now was spoke like good
People.

Thus we see from *Bull*'s Religious Character, from *Nurses* solemn acquiescence, and
from *Coupler*'s Reflection, the *Relapser* takes
Providence for *Divine* Appointment, and the
Pleasure of the first *Being.*

Berinthia comes again; and here the *Relap-*
ser has shown us what speed we may expect
from him when he strikes out. This Lady was
Worthy's Procuress. To succeed in her business she tells *Amanda, He* (Mr. Worthy)
used you like a Text, he took you all to pieces, but
spoke so Learnedly --- One might see the spirit of
the Church was in him. Now why does the
Vindicator deny his own Words, and affirm
the *Woman is not liken'd to a Text in general;* *Vind. P. 26*
or any other way? He had much better drop
the Cause, than plead it thus untowardly. To
return to the *Relapse. Berinthia* goes on in
Pulpit-phrase, and pursues her Employment
very intelligibly. At last she mentions *Use* *Relapse P.*
and Application, and brings them up to the *69.*
point of Debauchery. By her talking you
would think there was little Difference be-

I 2   tween

tween Lewdness and Religion. And that
Whoring and Preaching, a Church and a Baw-
dy-House might be treated alike. This fine
Discourse the *Vindicator*, out of his great Mo-
Vind.P.26 desty, calls *an inoffensive Simile, and says it abu-*
ses no body.

Berinthia concludes in Blasphemy, and joyns
the Atheist and the Procuress together. *Now
consider* (says she) *what has been said, and Hea-*
Relapse   *ven give you Grace to put it in Practise*; that is
Ibid.   to take *Berinthias* lewd Counsel, to prostitute
View, &c.   her Virtue, and turn Whore. These words
P. 84.   would be always Profane upon the *Stage*, but
the Application of them here, is flamingly
Blasphemous. The *Vindicator's* Defence is remarkable. He grants *these words are often u-*
P. 27.   *sed at the close of a Sermon, and therefore perhaps*
might as well have been let alone. It seems the
Case is somewhat doubtful, he is not sure but
that a Man may as well Blaspheme as let it a-
lone! One had need of Patience to read this.
Sr. Jude.   But St. *Michael* did not rail upon the Devil,
and therefore I shall pass it over. His lame
excuse from the *Character*, and *Manner*, I have
Relapse   disprov'd already. This *Berinthia* has a very
P. 49.   Scandalous Soliloquy ; She thanks heaven for
her Impudence, and is nauseously Bold, and
Profane : which, besides the Irreligion, is an
odd way of treating her Sex, and Figure.

We are now come to *the Abuse of the Clergy*. And here the *Vindicator's* method of purg-
ing himself is extraordinary. He runs a great
length of *Satyr* upon the Rights and Privileges
of the *Clergy*. I perceive the little Justice I
endeavoured to do that *Order*, won't down
with

with him. By his Reasoning one would think
the World strangely Priest Ridden, and all
Ages, Countrys, and Religions, extreamly
to blame! If you'll take his word for't, *Riches,
Plenty* and *Power*, are very Improper things p. 30.
for a Church-man. And yet this Gentleman
owns *the Institution of the Clergy to be the most
Effectual means of promoting our Happiness in this* Ibid.
World, and the other. Say you so? Then sure
they ought to have a share in the Common
Advantages. Acknowledgment should always
bear some Proportion to Obligation. Where's
the Gratitude, or even the Justice of acting
otherwise? If *Riches* and *Power* are things de-
sirable, why should not the *Clergy* come in
with the rest; If they are not, why are they
grudged them? To put the Priesthood under
a Disadvantage in the *State*, only for having
God's Commission, is an odd way of shewing
our Religion. 'Tis somewhat hard a Man
should be barr'd the Conveniencies of this Life,
for helping his Neighbours to a better. To
proceed. Are not the Clergy of the same
Humane Nature with other People? Have
they not the same Necessities for this World,
and the same Conscience and Discretion to
use it? Generally speaking, *Poverty* does as ill
with a *Priest*, as with a *Poet*. Tis apt to Sink
the Spirits, to make the Mind grow Anxious,
and Feeble in the discharge of Function. If
Riches are so invincibly dangerous, why don't
the Christian *Laity* part with them, and like
Crates, throw their Gold into the Sea? But
does not this Plea for the Churches *Temporals*,
reflect on the Author of Christianity; or as

the

the *Vindicator* too lightly expresses it, does.
it not suppose that *Christ and his Apostles*,
took the thing by the wrong handle ? By no means.
The case is not the same. The *Apostles* had a
Power of working Miracles, to hold up their
Character, and make way for their Doctrine.
They could Cure Diseases, and Inflict them ;
Kill and make Alive, Punish and Oblige in the
highest manner. They had Nature at their beck,
and Omnipotence about them. Such Credentials needed no other Recommendation. Such
Illustrious *Poverty* out-shines Imperial Gran-
deur, and makes a Cottage look Nobler than
a Court. But this Glorious Assistance was lent
but for a few Ages. When Christianity was
once Established, and Princes Converted to
the Faith, the end of Miracles went off, and the
Power was recalled. From this time the Church
was left in some measure to Humane Prudence,
and Civil Policy. When the Heavens were
thus shut in ; and the other World withdrew,
there was more occasion of recourse to This.
Now, Temporal Advantage, and Secular Sup-
port, grew much more seasonable, and the
Church was obliged to preserve her Authority by some of the methods of Civil Governours. But the *Vindicator* says, *Religion is not
a Cheat, and therefore has no need of Trappings*.
A Judge is no Cheat neither. 'Tis well known
he has a good Commission. To what purpose then are all these Formalities of the Court ;
All this Expence in Solemnity and Retinue?
Can't the Old Gentleman come like an *U-
topian Syphogranta*, with a wisp of Grass upon a Pole. Away, crys the *Vindicator*, with
all

*Vind. P.
30, 31.*

*Acts 3. 8.
& 5. 5, 10.
& 28. 8.
1 Cor. 5. 5.*

P. 32.

*Moor's
Utop.*

all this unnecessary State. Why must the *Charge* be given in *Furs* and *Scarlet*, when the Law will operate every jot as well in *Leather*? However, this Gentleman will have it that an *Ambassador who comes with advantageous Proposals, stands in no need of Equipage to procure him Respect.* This Project would save a great deal of Money? But there are few Princes of his mind. What does the *Vindicator* mean by all this good Husbandry? would he have an *Ambassador* Travel like a *Carrier* with a *Port-Manteau* behind him? Such Equipage would Represent strongly, and give a noble Idea of his business. In short, as things stand, Government of all kinds, requires somewhat of Figure. Appearance goes a great way in the Expediting of Affairs. Naked Reason won't always do. The generality must have their Senses struck, and their Imagination affected. Thus Authority is best refresh'd, and the Ends of the Institution secured. For this purpose Miracles were wrought; and when they cease, 'tis proper to apply to the usual Expedients.

And now I shall venture to confront the first *Article of his Heresy*, as he calls it, with this Truth, *viz. That the Shepherd who has least Meat at home in his House, has most Business:* For Indigence has a very working Head; and a Man is always most full of Care, when he does not know how to live: And for the same Reason, he that has the best Fortune, may be most at leisure, because he has others to manage his Affairs.

Ibid.

Vind. P. 31

I 4   The

The Vindicator in his 2*d.* Article difcourfes of *Sauce* and *Sops,* &c. But he has cook'd the Allegory fo oddly, that I know not well what to make on't. If he reafons from the Kitchin upon thefe fubjects, he muft talk by himfelf. His 3*d.* Article I have fpoken to already, and am now to confider it farther. For

The *Vindicator* pretends, That *Piety, Learning, Charity and Humility, would fecure the Clergy from Neglect, much better than Power, and Revenue.* Upon a View of the whole, one and t'other will be found to do very well together. For 1*ſt.* If Piety and Power are not to be reconcil'd, and a Man muft either throw up his Fortune or his *Creed,* the Laity will be oblig'd to the fame Refignation. The Inclofures of Property and Privilege muft be broken down, and all Things laid in Common. But if 'tis poffible for a Man to be Pious with a Penny in his Pocket, the Clergy I fuppofe may be fo, with as little difficulty as their Neighbours. Then as for *Learning,* Poverty, and this Advantage are inconfiftent. As the World goes, there's little Knowledge to be had without Money. A Man may get Honefty for nothing; but if he will have any Senfe to't more than ordinary, he muft pay for't. There are fome few Exceptions to this Rule, but generally fpeaking, it holds true. To go on. *Charity* is much better exercifed with *Revenue,* than without it. 'Tis true, a Beggar may have as large a Soul as a Prince. Bnt Will without Power, is neither fo clear nor fo ferviceable. He that can go no farther than a good Wifh, is oftentimes only kind in his Confcience, and

a Benefactor to himself. For where the Heart
is invisible, the Obligation must be so too.
But Power brings secret Goodness into Light,
and makes it appear unquestionable. And to
come closer to the subject, I believe if the
Preacher could Dine all the Poor of the *Parish*
every *Sunday*, his Sermon would be more significant. His Table would assist his Pulpit,
and his Charity reinforce his Reasoning.
They'd first come to him for the *Loaves*, and
then for the *Doctrine*. And lastly, as for *Humility*, I agree with the *Vindicator*; I think it
most necessary; and that no Man can be a
Christian without it. But whether I have the
same Notion of this Virtue with our Author
or not, I can't tell. To be humble, a Man is
bound not to be full of himself, or grow stiff
upon any Advantage, but give all the Glory
to God. He must be fair in Conversation, not
despise the least Mortal, but rather stoop
to oblige those upon lower Ground. Thus
far without doubt all Clergymen, and all
Christians are concern'd to be Humble.
But to be servile and sheepish to humour
Pride, and blow up Conceit, this is quite
another thing. There's neither Humility,
Discretion, nor so much as Honesty, in such
Management. 'Tis little Knavery, and para-
sitical Meanness; and Church Men, of all
People, should stand clear of so uncreditable
an Imputation. Now 'tis this sort of Humility
the *Stage* would put upon them. The *Vindi-*
cator and Mr. *Congreve*, are wonderfully for an
humble Clergy: And so are some of the
proudest Men I ever met with. If 'tis said the

Congr.
Amend.

Clergy

Clergy are bound to be *Exemplary*, I willingly
grant it. But Example fuppofes other Perfons
concern'd befides thofe who Set it. If the
Clergy are to be Examples, 'tis becaufe the *Lai-*
ty are bound to follow them : And in Humility too, as well as in other Duties. For if the
Teachers are bound to be Humble, the *Hearers*
without queftion are under the fame Obligation. The Argument might be prefs'd farther, but I rather chufe to leave it with the
Reader. And fince we are on the fubject of
Humility, the *Vindicator* and Mr. *Congreve*
would do well to think on't. If as this Gentleman obferves, *He who teaches Piety and Mo-*
rality to the World, is a great Benefactor to Man-
kind : Then by the rule of Contraries, he who
teaches Immorality, muft be as great a Nu-
fance. He who makes it his bufinefs to exter-
minate Vertue, and Confcience, and debauch
both Practice and Principle, muft needs be a
Misfortune to the Age. Unlefs they can clear
themfelves of this Imputation, they ought to
be wonderfully modeft and unpretending. To
be the Author of irreparable Mifchief ; to
deftroy the Innocence of Life, the Securities
of Government, and the Expectations of the
World to come, are powerful Reafons for
Humility. Thofe who in any meafure lye under this Charge, can hardly bend too low, or
think themfelves leffer than really they are.

Prov.Wif.   The *Vindicator* would make us believe, that
p.45,46, Sir *John Brute*'s debauching in a *Gown*, was no
51, 52.   Abufe of the Clergy. That's Strange ! I
View, &c. take it the Company were merry with the
180.   Difguife. 'Twas the Habit and Function which
                              made

made the Scene diverting. The Oaths and Lewdness would not have made half the Musick in a Lay-Character: And the *Constable's* Jests would have been but heavy upon another occasion. Besides. Sir *John* is made to abuse his pretended Brethren, and the Justice falls in general upon the *Order*. And is it no Disservice to be thus executed in Effigie, and made a Mad-man by *Representation?* If a Lewd Person could steal his Neighbour's Shape, and then play all his Pranks in't, I suppose he would have no Thanks for his pains. When the Badge of a Man's Office which should give him Credit, is shewn ridiculous, I fancy, he has reason to complain. If the *Vindicator* is of another mind, let him practise the same Liberty upon a *Judge*, or a *Lord Mayor*, and see how the Jest will take. Pro. Wife, 45,51.

I observ'd upon the *Relapse*, that *Bull* the Chaplain, wish'd the married Couple Joy, in Language horribly Smutty and Profane. I confess, I could not go on with it. And what says the *Vindicator* to this? Why he plucks up his Spirits, and lays it all upon the Board; no body could have transcrib'd a foul passage more honestly. And now who would suspect the Man to be otherwise than Innocent? Thus some People when they are going to put a Trick upon you, strip their Arm bare, and pretend strongly to fair Dealing. But here the matter was too gross for a cleanly Conveyance. To argue this Point any farther, would be an ill Compliment to the *Reader*, and therefore I shall pass it over. I charg'd the *Relapse, Preface* and *Play*, with a great deal more View, &c. 109.
Relap. 74.

Page 35.

View, &c.
109, 110,
232.

more scandalous Abuse of the *Clergy* ; but this
the *Vindicator* is pleas'd to overlook.   And as
to the irreligious Part, he only says, *'tis just*
as profane as the rest ; which though it may not
come up to the Merits of some passages, is
Character bad enough in all Conscience.

We are now advanc'd to a new *Chapter*.
And here the Vindicator would fain know
which way I make it appear, *That* Constant
is his Model for a Fine Gentleman ; and that he is
brought upon the Stage for Imitation.   This de-
mand is easily satisfyed.   That he stands for a
fine Gentleman, is evident from his Sense, his
Breeding, and his Figure? Now these Circumstances, with the fair Treatment he meets with,
make him a *Model* for *Imitation.*   This confe-
quence follows naturally from the Advantage
of his Character. For most young People of
any pretences, love to be counted fine Gentle-
men.   And when Vice has Credit, as well as
Pleasure annext, the Temptation is dange-
rously fortified.

The *Vindicator* tells the Reader, *That this*
honest Dr. does not understand the Nature of Co-
medy, tho he made it his Study so long. For the bu-
siness of Comedy is to shew People what they should
do, by representing them doing what they should not
do. Nor is there any Necessity to explain the Moral
to the Audience.   For all this Liveliness, I'm
afraid this honest Poet, neither understands
Comedy, nor himself, and that's somewhat worse.
Not himself, because he contradicts what he
wrote before. For in the beginning of his *Vin-*
dication he acquaints us how careful he was to
explain the *Moral*, for fear of misconstruction.

Yes ;

Page 35.

Page 44.

Page 45.

Vind. p 9.

Yes; for fear the *Boxes* and *Pit* should misinterpret him. But now the Tale is quite turn'd, Page 45. and there's no need of a Philosopher to unriddle the Mystery.

2*ly.* He mistakes the *Nature* of *Comedy.* This we may learn from *Ben. Johnson,* who acquaints the *University, That he has imitated the Conduct* Fox Ep. *of the Antients: In whose Comedies the Bawds,*&c. Ded. *yea and oft-times the Masters too, are multed, and that fitly,* it being the Office of a Comick Poet *to imitate Justice, and instruct to Life.* Is it the Office of a Comick Poet to *imitate Justice,* &c. then certainly Rewards and Punishments ought to be rightly apply'd: Then a Libertine ought to have some Mark of Disfavour set upon him, and be brought under Discipline and Disgrace. See View, To say the *Business of Comedy is to shew People* &c. 151, *what they should do, by representing them doing* 153,164. *what they should not,* is a pleasant way of arguing! What is the Stage to be read Backwards, and construed by Contradiction? When they talk Smut must we understand them in a Sense of Modesty; and take all their Profaneness for Pious Expression? Then by the same Rule, when they say any thing that's good, we must conclude they have a Lewd Meaning. This is an admirable Compass to Sail by; such Piloting must needs discover all the Rocks and Quick-sands in the Voyage! This undistinguishing Method at the best, would be like pulling up the Buoys, quitting the Helm, and leaving the Passengers to Steer at their Discretion. But as the Poets manage the matter, 'tis still more dangerous. For to shew a *Religious Person* ridiculous; to give Figure and Success

to

to an ill Character, and make Lewdneſs Modiſh and Entertaining, is the way to miſmark the Nature of Good and Evil, and confound the Underſtandings of the Audience. 'Tis the way to hide the *Flaws* in Behaviour, to Varniſh the *Deformity*, and make the *Blemiſhes* look Shining. The *Vindicator* inſiſts, *That* Conſtant *ſays nothing to juſtifie the life he leads, except,* &c. What needs he? He is ſufficiently juſtified in his Character and Uſage, and in not being puniſh'd. Let's have the reſt. *He does not juſtifie the Life he leads, except where he's pleading with Lady* Brute *to debauch her, and ſure no body will ſuppoſe him there to be ſpeaking much of his mind.* Why not? Does a Man who argues againſt Conſcience, and talks like an Atheiſt, never ſpeak his Mind? If a Libertine pleads in his own Defence, why muſt he not be ſuppos'd to be in earneſt? Beſides, how could *Conſtant* expect to carry the Cauſe, unleſs the Colours look'd fair, and the Reaſoning probable? To give this Spark his due, he makes the moſt of his Matters. He endeavours to inform the Lady, *That Virtue conſiſts in Goodneſs and Pity, not in ſnarling ſtraitlaced Chaſtity. That Honour is a phantome, and that the Importance of it lies in the Cuſtom of the Country, not in the Nature of the Thing* ; and pretends precedents for a *contrary Practice.* In ſhort, *Hobs* and *Spinoſa* could ſcarcely have ſaid more for him. This is admirable inſtruction! And *Lady Brute* for all the ſhrewdneſs of *her Anſwers*, confeſſes her ſelf *puzzl'd*, and ſuffers the Intrigue to go on. In a word, if the *Young Ladies* (the Vindicator takes ſuch care of) have nothing but this *Dia-*

logue

Vind. p. 46

Page 47.

Pro. Wife, Page 34.

ibid.

Pro. Wife, 35.

logue for their Security, I should think them in a dangerous Condition. And here I can't but take notice how the *Vindicator* contradicts himself again. He makes the Lady turn *Philosopher*, and gives an *Interpreter to the Poppet-Show*. Vind.p.47 Vind.p.45 47.

I tax'd his *Bellinda* for confessing her Inclination to a Gallant. For this he calls me *an unfair Adversary*, as if I had misreported him, adding withall, that *Bellinda* only says, *If her Pride should make her Marry a Man she hated, her Virtue would be in danger from the Man she lov'd.* His Play will soon decide this Controversy, and shew on which side the Unfairness lies. *Bellinda's* words are these: View, &c. 146. Page 47. Vind.p.48

Bellind. to Lady Brute. O' *my Conscience were it not for your Affair in the Ballance, I should go near to pick up some odious Man of Quality yet, and only take poor Heartfree for a Gallant.* This very *Bellinda* a little before advises Lady *Brute* to surrender her Virtue to *Constant.* The Lady requites her in a suitable encouragement. Prov. Wif. q. 64. Prov. Wif. p.45.

Lady Br. If you did commit Fornication Child, 'twou'd be but a good friendly part, if 'twere only to keep me in Countenance whilst I commit --- So it seems, she must turn Whore out of good Breeding. These two Ladies, in a private Dialogue, where we must suppose their Hearts are open, are extreamly instructive and civil to their Sex! *Lady Brute* informs her Neece, that the Men are most of them Atheists, and believe the Women to be no better; that by a Woman of *Reputation*, is meant no more than a Woman of *Discretion.* To this Accusation the Lady pleads Guilty, and confesses, *That want of Inclination* Ibid.

clination seldom protects any of her Sex. And as for *Fear,* 'tis too weak a Restraint to hold them long. And were it not for their Cowardise, they would likewise venture upon all the Masculine Vices of *Fighting, Swearing, Blaspheming,* &c. Here you have the Secrets of the *Cabinet,* and Truth and Ceremony in abundance. This Author in his *Vindication* Courts the *Sex* in his own Person. *With all due Respects* (says he) *to the Ladies, a Bishoprick may prove as Weighty a Reward, as a Wife, or a Mistress either.* It seems then in the Scale of this Civil Gradation, a *Mistress,* that is a Strumpet, is a weightier Reward than a Wife. Truly I think the *Vindicator* pays his *Respects* to the Ladies in this place, almost as untowardly as he did to the Devil before.

Prov.Wif.
P. 65.

Vind. p.44
45.

To conclude with the Provok'd Wife. The Men of Figure in this *Play,* (excepting the Justice, who makes but a short Enter) are profess'd Libertines, and pass off without Censure or Disappointment. I grant Sir *John's* Character has some Strokes of Discouragement, but he's made pretty easy at last, and brought to no Pennance. The Women have some of the same Inclinations; and the same good Luck with them. 'Tis true *Lady Fanciful* miscarries in her Design; has her Disguise pull'd off, and falls under some Confusion. But then we are to take notice, that this Lady was the most Modest of the Company. What e're her Thoughts were, she has the Discretion to keep them in Reserve. This Squeamishness, 'tis possible, drew down the Severity of the *Poet.* Had she been as bad as the rest, she might

Prov.Wif.
P. 76,77.

might have fared better. But it seems, a pretence to Virtue is an unsufferable Boldness ; and
she must be punish'd *in Terrorem* to her Sex.

This sort of Management puts me in mind of
Mr. *Dennis*'s Ingenuity. He frankly Confesses
Lewdness promoted by the *Stage*. This is clear
dealing : And I suppose, the main Reason of his
saying that the *Play-House* Contributes so much
to the Happiness of the Nation.

We are now come forward to the *Remarks* upon the *Relapse*. And here the *Vindicator* does as
good as confess he has *made many foolish Mistakes* Vind.P.56
in his Play. And by a peculiar happiness in 57.
his Understanding ; seems both sensible, and satisfied with it.

The *Vindicator* pretends much to Morals and
Instruction about *Loveless* and *Amanda* ; but can't
forbear running upon the old *Haunt*. For after
having made himself Merry with a *Venison Pasty
and a Tankerd of Ale* ; he falls a quoting the *Lords-* P. 61.
Prayer about his *Play*, and in different Characters, to make us sensible of his Devotion.

He goes on in the Relation of his *Fable*, quotes
Lead us not into Temptation once again ; and says,
Loveless had no farther occasion for that Petition. P. 65.
I wish the *Poet* is not of *Loveless*'s Opinion. His
making bold with so Solemn a Sentence upon so
light a Subject, is somewhat to be suspected.

He informs us that *Loveless* and *Amanda's
Virtue was built upon a Rock, and raised upon the* P. 65, 69.
utmost strength of Foundation, and had Religion,
&c. *to defend it.* And yet this *Pious* Couple are Relapse.P.
for *Mahomets* Paradise, and wish for Immortal 2, 3.
Sensualities.

K   He

He would make *Lovelef* and *Amanda* the
chief *Characters by the Importance of the Defign. The
Importance of his Play is Diverfion*; And to gain
This he has broke through the Rules of the *Drama*. But let his Private Defign be what it will,
I ftill fay, *Young Fafhion, Lord Foppington,* and
their Party, make the principal Figure in the
Play: The Plot, the Fortune, and the Conclufion, the greateft part of the *Play*, and of the
Perfons too is on their fide. As for poor *Lovelef* he finks in the middle of the *Fourth Act*, and
you may go look him. Here the *Vindicator*
could not find in his heart to quote fair; however, he makes a fhift to fay *that if the* Play
*had funk in the Fourth Act too, it had been bet-
ter than 'tis by juft Twenty* per Cent. If he does
not mean Pounds, I agree with him, fo far as
to own that if it had funk in the *Third Act* it had
been more Valuable. For fome *Entertainments*
like Dirty way, are always the better for being
fhort. However, does not this Confeffion prove
the Truth of my *Remarks*, and that *Lovelef* was
a Character of inferiour Confideration? Does
the main Concern ufe to die fo long before the
Epilogue, and the Cheif Perfon go off when about
a *Third* of the *Play* is remaining?

The *Vindicator* gives a Home Thruft at
Parting, but his Weapon like *Scaramouchy's* is
made of a *Rufh*. He complains mightily of *unfair Dealing*, and pretends I have Ridiculed the
Morality of the Scene between *Worthy* and *A-
manda*. Thus he endeavours to *caft a Mift* before the *Reader*, but a Man muft have bad Eyes
not to fee through it: For in this Reflection
upon *Worthy*, I was not examining the *Moral*,
but

P. 71.

Vind.P.60

P. 72.

P 73, 74.

but the *Dramatick* Virtues of his *Play*. This was
so plain that 'twas impossible for the *Vindicator* View. &c
P. 2 8,
to overlook it. I say my *Remarks* in this place 226, 227.
were only upon the *Manners* in a *Poetick* Sense.
My business here was to shew the Inconsistency
of *Worthy*'s Character, and the unlikelyhood of
his Reformation, indeed what can be more im-
probable than so suddain a change in behaviour ?
This Spark immediately before his Lecture of Relapse p.
Philosophy had told *Amanda* that *Sin no more was* 100.
a Task too hard for Mortals. This by the way, Joh. 3. 11.
is a bold Contradiction of our *Saviour*, 'tis Impious in the Assertion, and Lewd in the Appli-
plication ; So few words can hardly be charged with more Profaneness. Here the *Relapser*
calls the Sense of the *Scripture* in question, charges the *Text* with Untruth, and does that which Vind. P. 14
by his own Confession amounts to *Burlesque*.

To return to *Worthy*, what can be more im-
probable than that so Profane and finished a *De-*
bauchee, so weak in Principle, and so violent in
Passion, should run from one extream to another ? Should break through Custom, and me-
tamorphose Desire at so short a warning ? To
Solicit to Rudeness, and talk Sentences and Morality, to be Pious and Profane in the same
Breath must be very extraordinary. To be all
Pleasure and Mortification so just together, a
Mad-man one Minute and a Hermit the next,
is one would think somewhat forced, and un-
natural : It looks at best but like the Grimace
of a Disappointment, the *Foxes* virtue when the
Grapes were above his Reach. To make a Libertine talk like *Plato*, or *Socrates*, is Philosophy misplac'd, 'tis good advice, but out of Character,,

racter ; The Soil and the Plant, the Man and
the Morals won't agree.

Thus it appears the *Blot* he makes so much
a noise with, lies in his own *Tables* ; whether
I have hit it, or not, the *Reader* must judge.
I am glad to hear him talk of *his Grave* : 'Twas
a seasonable Thought, and I heartily wish it its
due improvement ; Such a Consequence wou'd be
of great service, both to himself and the Publick. For then, I am well assured, he would
neither Write *Plays*, nor Defend them, at the
rate he has done.

I have nothing farther with the *Vindicator* ;
but before I Conclude, I shall speak to one Objection proposed by the *Defender of Dramatick Poetry*, and Mr. *Dennis*. These Authors endeavour
to justifie the *Theater* from the Silence of the
Scriptures. " The Word of God (say they) has
" no where condemned *Plays*, the *Apostles* who
" were particular in other Cases, have given
" the *Stage* no Reprimand, nor Christians any
" warning against it : And which is more,
" St. *Paul* makes no Difficulty in citing *Menan-
" der* a Comick *Poet*, which he would not have
" done unless he had approved both the Au-
" thor and his business too. This is the sum
of what they offer. Now the Plea of St. *Paul's*
citing *Menander*, is extreamly slender. Every
foreign Sentence in *Scripture* is not commended
by the bare mention. The Devil's Maxim of
Skin for Skin, &c. is set down, but not for our
Imitation. I grant this Verse of *Menander* is
Moral, and Sententious ; And without doubt
St. *Paul*

P. 73, 74.

P. 78.

Defence of
*Dramat.
Poetry* P.
40, 43, 55,
56.
The Use-
fulness of
the Stage,
P. 138,
139. &c.

Job 2. 4.

St. *Paul* cited it to put the Chriſtians upon their Guard, and that they might be aſham'd to fall ſhort of the Inſtructions of the *Heathens*. But to infer that St. *Paul* approved all that *Menander* had written, and that the *Apoſtle* recommended *Plays* to the *Corinthians :* To conclude all this from one ſingle Line of Quotation, is Prodigious conſequence. This Latitude would juſtifie the *Stage* to purpoſe, and make the Lewdeſt Authors paſs Muſter. There being few Books ſo entirely Vitious as not to afford an inoffenſive and ſignificant period. I don't ſpeak this with application to *Menander*, for as *Plutrarch* obſerves, he was with reſpect to *Ariſtophanes*, a very Modeſt *Poet*. Beſides this very quotation *that evil communication corrupts good Manners*, diſſerves the purpoſe 'twas brought for. 'Tis a ſharp Rebuke of the Licentiouſneſs of our *Stage*, and a plain Diſcountenance of ſo ſcandalous a Diverſion.

To proceed with the Objection. I affirm that *Plays* are plainly condemned in *Scripture* upon two accounts. I ſay they are clearly condemned, tho not by expreſs Prohibition ; yet by Principle and Conſequence, which is the ſame thing.

1. They are condemned upon the ſcore of *Idolatry* ; They were parts of *Pagan* Worſhip, and under that notion unlawful to Chriſtians. But this Reaſon expiring in a great meaſure with the *Heathen* Religion, I ſhall inſiſt on it no farther. However it proves thus much, that the Unlawfulneſs of every Liberty is not particularly Mark'd in *Scripture*. For in the *Apoſtles* time, Mr. *Dennis* allows *Plays* were Idola-

P. 141, 142.

trous

trous and unlawful ; and yet we see the Holy *Text*
does not declare against the *Theater* by Name.

2. The *Stage*, (particularly the *English* one)
is condemned in *Scripture* upon the score of Smut
and Profaneness ; upon the Account of the *Danger* and Indecency of such Liberties. We are
strictly commanded in *Scripture not to Swear at
all, to put away all Blasphemy and filthy Communication out of our Mouth* ; *.To serve God with Reverence, to be Sober and Vigilant. To pass the time
of our sojourning here in fear, and abstain from all
appearance of Evil.* And in a word, *To have no
pleasure in* Scandalous Practices, *no fellowship with
the unfruitful works of Darkness, but rather reprove
them.* Here's Evidence enough in all reason,
these Admonitions are full against our *Stage*. Not
one *Play* in forty can stand the *Test* of so much
as one single *Text*. Bring the *Theater* but to
the *Bible*, and the Idol is presently discovered,
and falls like *Dagon* before the *Ark*.

This Argument from the silence of our *Saviour* and his *Apostles* is answered at large by the
Bishop of *Meaux* in his late Book against the
Stage. Which being so much to the Purpose, I
shall Translate it for the *Reader*.

"Those (says he) who would draw any Advantage from this Silence may by the same
"reason defend the Barbarities of the *Gladiators*,
"and other abominable *Spectacles*, which are all
"unmentioned in *Scripture*, no less than *Plays*.
"The Holy Fathers who have dealt with this
"Objection, will furnish us with Matter for a
"Reply, we say then, That all engaging Representations which excite, and fortifie unlawful
"Desires, are condemned in *Scripture*, together
"with

Margin notes:
St. Mat. 5.
James 5.
Ephes. 5.
Collos. 3.
Heb. 12.
1 Pet. 1.
1 Pet. 5.
1 Thes. 5.
Rom. 1. 32
Eph. 5. 11.

1 Sam. 5. 3.

Maximes
& Reflections sur
la Comedie. P. 71,
&c.

" with the Vices they tend to. For the purpose,
" Lewd Pictures are censured by all those Paf-
" sages which declare in general against Im-
" modesty; And the same may be said of *Dra-*
" *matick* Representations. St. *John* has compre-
" hended the whole of this Subject in the fol-
" lowing Injunction. *Love not the world, neither*
the things that are in the world : If any man love I Jo. 2. 15.
the world, the love of the Father is not in him. For
all that is in the world, is the Lust of the flesh, and
the lust of the eyes, and the pride of Life, which Lust
or Concupiscence, *is not of the Father, but of the*
World. " Now if these Things, and Inclina-
" tions, *are not of God,* the moving Representa-
" tions, and Charming Images of them, are not
" of *Him* neither, but *of the World* ; and by
" consequence Christians have nothing to do
" with them.

" St. *Paul* likewise has summ'd up the Argu-
" ment in these words. *Finally my Brethren, what-*
soever things are true, whatsoever things are honest,
whatsoever things are just , whatsoever things are Phil. 4. 8.
pure, (or according to the Greek whatsoever things
are chast) whatsoever things are lovely, whatsoever
things are of good report ; if there be any virtue, or
if there be any praise, think on these things. " As if
" he had said, whatever hinders you from think-
" ing on these things, and possesses you with
" contrary Amusements, ought not to be en-
" tertained as a Pleasure, but suspected as dan-
" gerous. In this beautiful collection of Thoughts
" which St. *Paul* recommends to a Christian,
" there's no finding a Place for the Modern *Thea-*
" *ater,* how much soever it may be in the favour
" of some Secular People.

" Far-

"Farther, The Silence of our Saviour upon
"the Argument of *Plays*, puts me in mind that
"he had no occasion to mention them to the
"*House* of *Israel*, to which he was sent, these Di-
"versions being never admitted in that Nation.
"The *Jews* had no *Shews* to entertain them but
"their Feasts, their Sacrifices, and their Holy
"Ceremonies. They were form'd by their Con-
"stitution to a plain and natural way of Living;
"They knew nothing of these Fancies and Inven-
"tions of *Greece :* So that to the praises which
"*Balaam* gives them, that *there is no Enchantment*
"*in Jacob, nor Divination in Israel*; We may like-
"wise add, there was no Theater among them;
"nothing of these dangerous Amusements to be
"met with. This innocent undebauch'd People,
"took their Recreations at Home, and made their
"Children their Diversion. Thus after their
"Labours in the Fields, and the Fatigues of their
"Domestick Affairs; they reliev'd their Spirits,
"as their Patriarchs had done before them. In-
"deed if we consider the matter rightly, there's
"no need of making a Business of Pleasure? Na-
"ture is easily refresh'd without this Expence and
"Curiosity.

"The Apostle's saying nothing expresly on
"this Subject may possibly be resolv'd into the
"reason abovemention'd. These Holy Men be-
"ing bred to the plain Gust of their Forefathers,
"might not think themselves concern'd to write
"directly against those practices with which
"their Nation was unacquainted : 'Twas suffici-
"ent for them to lay down Principles by which
"such Liberties were discountenanced : The
"Christians were well satisfied their Religion
"was

Numb.
xxiii. 23.

" was founded on the Jewiſh, and that the *Church*
" never allow'd of thoſe Diverſions which were
" baniſh'd the *Synagogue.* But let the matter be
" how it will, this *Precedent* of the Jews reaches
" home to the Profeſſors of Chriſtianity. It be-
" ing a Shame that the *Spiritual Iſrael* ſhould in-
" dulge their Senſes in thoſe Pleaſures, which the
" *Carnal People* knew nothing of.

Before I diſmiſs the *Reader*, I'le juſt give him
a taſte of Mr. *Dennis*'s Skill and Modeſty in an-
ſwering a Teſtimony.

I cited *Plutarch* to ſhew the Opinion of the
Athenians concerning *Plays :* This People (ſays Plut. de
" he) thought *Comedy* ſo unreputable a perfor- Glo. Athe-
" mance, that they made a Law that no Judge of nienſ.
" the *Areopagus* ſhould make one. Here Mr. View, &c.
Dennis replies very roundly, *This Citation is abſo-* P. 240.
lutely falſe. Right ! 'Tis falſe in the *Latin*, but Dennis, P.
'tis true in the *Greek.* τὴν μὲν κωμῳδοποιίαν ὕτως 85.
ἄσεμνον ἡγοῦντο ᾐ φορτικὸν, ὥςε νόμῳ ἦν μηδένα ποιεῖν
κωμῳδίας ἀρεοπαγίτην. De Glor. Athen. p. 348.

Beſides, the *Latin* makes more againſt him.
For by that the Law ſays, *That no Man whatſoever* Dennis, p.
ſhould write any Comedys ; which is a higher Cen- 86.
ſure than the other. I hope, for the future Mr.
Dennis won't confide ſo much in a Tranſlation ;
eſpecially when it ſits harder than the *Original.*

His Remark from *Ariſtotle*'s Treatiſe of *Poetry*
is another Miſtake ; and I think not at all to his
Advantage : But to ſet him in his way , this
Philoſopher does not ſay that *Comedy was very*
much diſcourag'd at firſt, nor very little neither.
This point was not argued : He only affirms, Ariſt. lib.
That it was a great while before the Chorus was fur- de Poet.
niſh'd out by the Government. cap. 5.

I

I ſhould now go on with Mr. *Dennis,* and ſhew his Attempt on my other Authorities as unſucceſsful as this upon *Plutarch*; but having ſome Buſineſs at preſent, I ſhall wave it till a farther Opportunity.

One word with the *Vindicator of the Stage*, and I have done.

This Gentleman appear'd early in the Cauſe, and has given me very little trouble, and therefore 'twould hardly be Civil not to diſpatch him at the firſt Hearing.

He pretends I miſtake in Tranſlating *Sæcularia Spectacula, Stage Plays.*

Vindic. P. 22,23.

View, &c. p. 250.

To this I Anſwer, Firſt, That I only affirm'd the *Stage* was manifeſtly comprehended under *Sæcularia Spectacula:* And that it is ſo, will follow from his own Aſſertion. For if the *Ludi Sæculares,* and *Sæcularia Spectacula* were the ſame, 'tis well known that *Stage Plays* were part of the *Ludi Sæculares;* all the *Theaters* being frequented at thoſe publick Solemnities.

Roſin. Schott. p. 757.

Secondly, The third Council of *Carthage* by me cited, can't poſſibly mean the *Secular Plays* by *Sæcularia Spectacula:* For this Council was held *anno* 397. fourſcore years and better after the Converſion of *Constantine.* Now theſe *Ludi Sæculares* were Idolatrous, both in the Practice and Inſtitution, and never celebrated after the Empire became Chriſtian: The laſt time we hear of them was in the Reign of the Emperor *Philip,*

Euſeb. in Chron.

a. 248. which was 149 years before the converting of this Council.

Thirdly, *Sæculum* and *Sæcularis,* in the Language of the Fathers, relates to the unconverted *World,*

World, in contradiſtinction to the *Church.* Thus
Typhus Sæcularis in the Life of *Arnobius,* ſignifies
Heathen Pride. And thus the Council inter-
prets it ſelf by calling theſe *Sæcularia Spectacula,* View, | P.
Pagan Entertainments. I almoſt wonder the *Stage-* 250.
Vindicator could cite the words and miſtake the
ſenſe.

What this Author may have farther, requiring
conſideration, he may find in my Reply to Mr.
Congreve, and the *Relapſer,* and thither I refer
him.

———————————

F I N I S.

A Short View of the Profaneness and
Immorality of the English Stage, &c.
Effays upon feveral Moral Subjects. 8º.

Both by Mr. Collier.